WHEN YOU LEARN THE ALPHABET

Winner of the Iowa Prize for Literary Nonfiction

WHEN YOU LEARN THE ALPHABET

KENDRA ALLEN

UNIVERSITY OF IOWA PRESS

IOWA CITY

University of Iowa Press, Iowa City 52242

www.uipress.uiowa.edu
Printed in the United States of America

Text design by April Leidig

Printed on acid-free paper

Library of Congress Cataloging-in-Publication Data
Names: Allen, Kendra, 1994– author.
Title: When you learn the alphabet / by Kendra Allen.
Description: Iowa City : University of Iowa Press, [2018] |
"Winner of the Iowa Prize for Literary Nonfiction." |
Identifiers: LCCN 2018032923 (print) | LCCN 2018052977 (ebook) |
ISBN 978-1-60938-630-6 (ebook) | ISBN 978-1-60938-629-0 (paperback : alk. paper)
Subjects: LCSH: Allen, Kendra, 1994–
Classification: LCC PS3601.L4322 (ebook) | LCC PS3601.L4322 A6 2018 (print) |
DDC 814/.6 [B] —dc23
LC record available at https://lccn.loc.gov/2018032923

Dedicated to Joe Budden's "Different Love."

The song I listened to most
when I needed help telling the truth
about my thoughts and myself.

She could hear him telling the mama that the girl had too much spirit,
that she had to learn to mind, that
that spirit had to be broken.

—bell hooks, *Bone Black*

CONTENTS

WHEN YOU LEARN THE ALPHABET

DARK GIRLS

My daddy's side of the family has blood made of craw daddies
bayou waters
red bones
big waves of silk

When I was born I came out looking just like them. I could pass as masta's daughter, just like them. The first picture I ever took fresh out of my mama's womb, looks just like them: a Louisiana Creole French-tongued thoroughbred. My eyes are closed so tightly you can see the wrinkles on my eyelids. I looked tired already. My hands are palm up, pressed closely to my ears at a few minutes old. I was born into surrender. My skin, almost the color of spoiled milk, thick and light all at the same time. Bubbling and burning, all at the same time

My mama wanted to name me Africa; as a symbol, just as much as a name. She knew I would fit the description. My mama, pronounced MawMaw—my daddy's mother—told me she knew my colorless world wouldn't last long when she looked at the back of my ears and it was only sundown, my downfall. She said she knew I would turn into nighttime before the sun set and rose again. I could tell she didn't want me to fit the description

Before my daddy planted seeds inside my almost too dark mama, he was told not to. Now he tells me there's no way any child I might house will have skin less potent than mine. He tells me even if the father is just as bright as him, my shadow will still cast itself upon my offspring. But I scrub off my curves. Stand up straight. Crack my own hips. I don't want anyone's grandchildren

People who love me but not my skin tell me at least I'm a pretty dark-skinned girl, an insult as salutation. My pretty dark-skinned girl smile doesn't translate to my pretty dark-skinned girl lips that could potentially appreciate the attention of someone who thinks they're giving me a gift by calling me a good colored girl / a negro girl / a dark girl / a violent girl / a black bitch / a field girl. I'm all of these things. I should say thank you. At least they don't lie

i am a reminder for them to say
at least I have
good child bearing hips
and a good spirit

maybe i'll attract a man like them
lighten up my offspring
teach them how to say *not enough* in French
dance to zydeco and suck juice right from the head of a crawfish

watch them turn red instead of purple like they mama

My Aunt Ceal called/calls me, *chocolate*. She'd say, *chocolate, when you gone come and see me?* Said, *look at chocolate*, whenever I was in her presence, made me aware of my chocolate, nicknamed my blackness, made me like the apparentness of my ash-prone tone, the burnt toast color of my brownness early on. Made me see the difference. I'd like to think she did it to train my spirit to stay inside my body when my complexion would inevitably began to be pointed out in place of a greeting. Train my mind to still be ok. Even if they never smile. Even if they look uncomfortable. I'd know she always smiled when she said it and it always felt like an attribute instead of a definition

When I was younger my skin was as smooth as it's ever gonna get. It gave me no problems. I did nothing for it but clean it with warm water. Never had a second thought about it. Didn't have any dark marks, discoloration, or confidence issues behind it. It was not a lump or a bruise covering it besides the mark on my thigh after being run over by my friend's bike. But I did notice there was something lurking in it I hadn't/haven't fully come to terms with. How much it hurts other people to see me while simultaneously trying to find a type of peace in knowing I wouldn't want to change my darkness even if I could. It came when I visited a dermatologist for my bad skin. It's been on a decline since I was a teenager—the aftermath of picking and itching at it for years. Peeling holes and creating scars that last too long. I got medicine to fix me. Months later the medicine turned my face the color of my father, my mawmaw, my nana. I was bleached back into a newborn from the neck up. It started out in blotches, on my chin, spaces in my cheeks. I thought I was experiencing a case of the michael jackson disease. I got scared. After a couple of weeks of using the medicines, the light eventually eased its way onto my whole face. Wiped me out completely. I looked like a ghost, like Casper, and the world began to look proud of me. I was always looking deep into mirrors trying not to search for a brightness, but a light. I didn't know I'd find it like this, I didn't know I'd immediately want to give it back

I've experienced two spectrums. One as the light-skinned girl deemed pretty just for being light-skinned. This lasted about three months before the medicine began to reverse me back into my original texture. I saw the way everyone reacted. Black men reacted. My men react. When I opened my front door during this time I could physically see them lose breath over my perceived beauty. It felt good. I covered the darker parts of my body that hadn't changed, my arms, my neck, my legs, in hoodies, in pants, in the required layering of the Chicago winds. Let only my face show for a few months. It felt good until I missed looking like something, until I missed looking like me, until I missed being behind the scenes. I know an opposite existence. One as the dark-skinned girl deemed pretty for being a dark-skinned girl. This will outlast anything. I see the way everyone reacts. Men react. Black men react, my men react, as if I'm not supposed to fit my description

The color of my skin is never trained to mean something different, something alternate, any more diverse, to anyone outside my race. They might see me as rich, but they still see black. They've never seen one of us, they just see all of us. They do not see caramel, yella bones, creole, good hair, bad hair, they most times see just a nigga. They don't see chocolate, bleaching creams, sunscreens, brown skin, light skin, they just see African. We see stained glass, three-fifths compromise in me. We see "Four Women" and Nina Simone's lips. We see a burning, an aftermath of sins. I know people who look at me like poor baby

When I go to a different dermatologist and show her what happened to my face she says *Well* . . . and pauses to figure out how to complete her thought professionally . . .

Well . . . she finishes this time . . . *Did you like it?*

I tell little girls who look like me their skin could persuade multitudes to make moves. That they are so beautiful. So beautiful. That you are beautiful. I move fast to protect them. I can't let them end up like me. They say they want to be like me. Ask me to be their play sister, their camp mother. Something in me makes me want to be my aunt. Even if I don't know if what I'm telling them is true enough to mean something

I tell them to develop a sharp tongue because you will be told directly or indirectly that you are an issue. That they'll start to see holes, a constant reminder they could be cuter if only they could shed like a reptile. I want to tell them they will be ok even when a parent inflicts the narrative on them. Tell them they'll be ok even when a boy they like only likes girls who don't look like her. Tell them they all will call it a preference for a long while instead of fixation, instead of a complex. Tell them they will all call it a preference instead of self-deprecation. I tell them they will be ok as time blesses them. I tell these little girls I love their hair, the way it stands, but this thing that covers their bones will always matter just a little bit more. I tell them good chocolate ain't never been cheap. I write to them. I write for them. Hope this helps them recover quicker than I did. I tell them they are not special occasions. I tell them to speak up even if they think you are already too loud because so much time will be spent in defense, I tell them to make it count

To consciously aware white men who like to use pet names to describe the varieties in our complexions: I am not your mocha frappe chocolate chip hand-dipped princess. I don't even drink coffee. Please stop

To white women who tan all day then use the word *ghetto* or *hood* or *rude* as a substitute for my blackness: you cannot be scared of me and then try to be the fun parts of me. You cannot burn yourself ragged to look like me. You cannot wear my essence and think you are above this black girl bad attitude

To light-skinned black men who seek me out. Who have held their arms out next to mine without judgment or delay. Who show me love like no other. Thanks for making me an object of your seduction, but you are not a prize I cannot give back. I don't know what you think this is, you are not doing me a favor

To light-skinned black girls who think their disposition grants them special access. Who think it's hard having skin that passes the paper bag test, who think it's hard being a pretty black girl because your whole life is just one big assumption, who can't help being helplessly pretty, I do not know what to tell you besides pretty girl, I cannot agree to make you feel good at the expense of me

To black men in general who are currently on a melanin kick because the internet told you it's cool to love yourself now, who pretend their darkness doesn't look just like mine. Fighting to prove you no longer long for the light-skinned black girls anymore, the mixed black girls anymore, the foreign but possibly black girls anymore, the racially ambiguous black girls anymore. Who calls me your favorite dark cousin instead of my name, you cannot treat me like a fad when I treat you like a treasure

Sometimes I wonder if all the black women in the world woke up one day and were cursed with black roses as covering, as lifelong armor, would we all be as uninviting in public when we look just like their mamas. I wonder could the women handle the pressure that comes with that partiality. It would be like having an infectious disease, scratching at their seams until the shade bursts open and turns back into sunlight. They would all fight and tug to get out as if there isn't room for us all

Nowadays I'm told *you not even that dark*. Nowadays,   I'm told the blacker the berry the sweeter the juice and dark skin is heritage and exotic and strong and black girl magic but all black girls weren't magic, some of us were curses who cast spells on God wishing to wake up four shades in the other direction

who hoped people they have been born of didn't use them as
containers for last resorts
then broadcast the truth as a self-esteem issue

because you look too much how
white people looked at their dirt how
when their blood was splattered across
acres of pain how
when they were forced to say yes sir

like black ain't black ain't black ain't black
like you can change it like
black ain't black ain't black ain't black
and the delusion that it's not is frightening
even when it's sad and immovable and it hurts

I thought about my aunt this year when I sat out in the sun on purpose. All day I stared at my legs changing colors and I fell asleep under the heat. I sweated. I melted. When I woke up, my arms and chest were the color of hell. My face the color of damn near charcoal. I got my first ever sunburn. I didn't care about getting darker than I already am. I didn't hear *girl you getting darker and darker*. I didn't hear *you sholl is getting black*. I didn't hear *you fine as hell, you just black as hell.* I didn't hear anything. I felt like I couldn't get black enough. Felt like I wasn't scared of the dark. Felt thankful for my body and its color. Felt like I wasn't sorry I can be a happy, scary, confusing sight, the way my skin gleams, shines, and soaks up every ounce of the hopes that were had for me. My taste buds glistening under chocolate moons, black as hell, dark as night, so black that when the lights are off all you can see are my teeth right before I take a bow

ABOUT AMERICAN MARRIAGES

In 1995, my mama and her two sisters—my aunts—are outside sharing a joint in the North Dallas projects. Their brother—my uncle—records them with his new camcorder, a piece of equipment that remained attached to his right hand throughout the late 90s and early 2000s documenting all of our childhoods. We know this because we watch these home videos almost every time we get together.

It's easy to notice how happy our parents used to be. Now they are just tryna maintain.

On this sweaty day, he zooms in on his sisters; their fingers wrapped around empty beer bottles, their clothes oversized hand-me-downs from one another, a real original girl group. They talk about the past, their adolescences, as my uncle pans to some of us kids who are chasing each other around our parent's wobbly feet, living out our own youths, our hair half done, our teeth still baby Chiclets, our voices only developed to form phrases instead of real sentences. We say *have candy* and *gotta pee*. We hold our hands above our heads when we get tired of using our feet. Our mamas call us their babies when they wipe the dried up juice from the corners of our mouths with their hands.

I don't see myself in this particular video, but when I see my daddy walk into the frame, I know I'm born. My parents are together. Something that only really happened at the beginning stages of my life. I'm already existing within something, within a union, that in my opinion, should have never existed. I'm at least a couple of weeks old; I'm probably just as new as that camcorder, the smell of Similac still on my breath. I stare at my daddy's cigarette-stained teeth, a habit he has yet to abolish. He is yelling in my uncle's direction. They talk about sports, about basketball. His Houston Rockets jersey is on full display, accompanied by a red and white Houston Rockets baseball cap. His face is yellow. He looks like the RCA cables you plug into the back of the TV. If I didn't know him, I would probably think he was of some Latino lineage. Compare his complexion to mine; it looks like I don't belong to him. He complains about Mexican women always tryna holla' speaking Spanish, and he tells them, *I don't speak that shit.* He resents Mexicans because he looks like one. Like me, he might resent a lot of things that remind him of who he is. But he's ranting into the camera with bleeding eyes as my mama passes him the joint for the third time. He's saying something about how Dallas ain't shit compared to *muhfuckin* Houston. I laugh during this part, at the sincerity behind his statement. You can tell he misses home. He misses his freedom. I interpret this as him reaching out for it whichever way he can.

Yet he has a smile on his face. I'm not sure if his smile is the: I'm so in love with my wife happiness or a depiction of a façade he likes to portray, because this is one of the only times I've seen him look like it isn't hurting him to be a part of this family, my family. Sisters and mamas and nieces and nephews hex his status as a husband. He isn't the center of my mama's world. Maybe only a tiny bit of this was showing in this video. Or maybe no one was looking hard enough. But I think this smile, on this particular day, is just the weed that has him all cheesy. Or possibly he is smiling because he and my mama are newlyweds. Newlyweds always smile. Probably because they have a lot of new, married sex they don't have to feel guilty about. It's "without sin," no matter how much we tend to sin in the midst of a pure thing anyway.

As he stands next to my mama, I realize I look just like her: same eyes, same stance, same hair type, all physicality. The camcorder captures the clouds of smoke suffocating them both, taking them under. Reminding me that even with all this, I have more in common with him: my nose, my character, my ego, my rage.

I watch my parents on the screen like they're an independent film—low budget—not enough nurturing or promotion to ever have a significant success rate. I watch them, together, a rare occurrence. It looks more like fun than love. If it is love I wouldn't know how to identify it. It looks more like lust and liability. All sex and no emotional development. I know there must be some, somewhere, but I've never cared to witness it.

I never watch them with any expectations; I already know their ending. I watch them like a warning.

Almost ten years post their divorce, when I'm fresh out of my teens and teetering on the precipice of young adulthood, my mama makes an announcement at my uncle's house that she never wanted to be married. That although she was in love, marriage was never the goal for her. I don't tell her I think marriage shouldn't be the goal for any two people, instead I ask her why did she stay married when what I really wanted to ask was why didn't she leave before he did. Somehow everything is always a competition with me, even who leaves who. But I'm asking because I'm hoping she will not say she stayed married because of me.

She says it just seemed like the next step to take because he asked.

I don't tell her how I'm all for fornication and broken homes and how I think they make independent women seeing as how we're both products of this recipe. I don't ask her why she never acknowledged her home would be broken into anyways whether she was married or not. I don't tell her how this information makes me look at her differently, gives me room to make her decision-making about me.

During the time her marriage was failing / had failed, my mama cried all the time for a long time. She would lock herself in the closet to do so and I'd come knocking on the door, let the wood scrape and burn against my knuckles because I was bored and an only child and needed someone to play with and she was gone too long. I would talk to her through the door thinking she was hiding from me. Sometimes she would answer depending on what I said. Most times she would tell me to go back and watch TV. But I would always come back and knock again until she came out:

mama!
mama!
mama!
mama! in my small,
annoying little kid voice
repeatedly until she cracked
open the door to tell me, once again,
she'd be out in a
minute.

And I would wait,
and she would always come out ready to play.

Later on in my life, she tells me she was praying all those nights.

I don't tell her how much I used to pray during those times too. Praying for God to take me out the middle of grown folk's business.

This is what happened: What I've been told: Which is what always happens: Your husband begins having sex with a woman who isn't you and he doesn't even care enough to hide it well. There is nothing special or innovative about it. It's nothing more than an American pastime within an American love story with no love and if the love is there it's based on too many conditions.

First, it's just your intuition telling you. Then, after you put him out of the house and he moves in with his brother, you and your child come over to do laundry one night while he's out. You find a card on the top shelf in the kitchen from a woman who isn't you with words like love and happiness handwritten between the empty spaces. Mostly love. That's what sets you off, love, because you asked and he lied and you thought your husband loved you. Next, you find condoms under his bed and a pair of panties. You are not bombarded by this discovery completely. You already know, which is why he's no longer in your home. So you write down the address from the card of forbidden love and you drive yourself, your child, and the dog to the woman who loves your husband's house. It's a nice neighborhood. Close-knit.

On the other side of town. When you ring her doorbell, a small child answers the door—a child your own child will eventually grow to know, and like, and share memories with. You tell the child at the door to go get her mama. When this woman who loves your husband walks to the door, you think she doesn't seem that surprised to see you there. She verifies all the things said in the letter for you.

You drive back to the apartment where the man the two of you share on occasion lives and finish washing your clothes. When you're done, you take his house keys back to your house. It's petty but you know he will come for them. You don't tell your husband you know his secret. You know eventually she will, if she hasn't already.

When he comes for the keys, you're silent as you hand them off through the half cracked open door, closing it just as quickly when he says *that's what you get.*

You repeat what he said *that's what I get?*

He says, *yea, for being nosy.*

Soon after this you find out your husband is not only having an affair, but he's having one with a woman who works in the same hospital building as ya'll. You find this out because she walks by your desk.

You work on the first floor.
She works somewhere close by.
He works under the both of you.

For the past few months, you've been seeing a psychiatrist to talk to someone about him, about you, about this, about disability, about abandonment, about all your issues. You don't tell your husband what you've been doing. You don't tell him because you don't trust him. This is your one secret to keep.

One day, your husband mentions he knows. He begins to say things to you like: *that's why you crazy* and *doctors* and *medication* and *you must not be taking your pills*. You ask him where he heard this from. No one can convince you it's not her. You don't know how but she's been telling him everything else. He denies just like a husband should.

You don't care much at this point that your marriage is ruined; it's more about the principle. It's not about him or about her. You say she can have your husband, but she can't be telling him your business, which is why you tell your boss.

When my mama tells me this, I think she's lying. It sounds too much like a movie—a romantic comedy—big budget—predictable plot. Only in movies does the wife confront the other woman. But I listen like an avid moviegoer, wishing I could yell at the screen and tell her to stop while she was ahead, to yell that there are more important things than continuing to love the wrong man. That there are more important things than men period. That she is not the first or last woman this will happen to. No one sees the underlying message of the storyline, the utter cliché of it all, the redundant narrative or boring boy/girl shit, but me.

After what I assume is a breakup, my parents stay separated, but connected, for seven more of my childhood years. I don't understand why. We don't have any assets or property or savings so divorce ain't that expensive. All it costs is a child. But legally separated is the title they go with. I don't know if this means single. I think it means continuing to thread a knot of possession around something that strings you along, around something that is trying to get away. I think it means something that lacks finality. It means single to my daddy but my mama's heart is still in it, still hopeful, and it's probably because he lets her think there's some left. She is not yet ready to fully let go of this idea of family even if I'm the one stuck in the middle of it.

To see her navigate through it you'd think she's Superman—because she acts like Superman. I think she's Superman too, but without the superpowers and I spend my time trying to fix her.

At the start of this seven-year separation, my daddy immediately moves back to Houston but he's still in contact with his wife. The two of them are still in heat. My mama says a married man is always still having sex with his wife, even when distance is a factor. My daddy comes and goes from bed to bed: one that is legally binding and another that is made on broken commandments. He is living a bachelor life with a wedding ring in storage. He comes to town to meet his real wife at random hotels, in secret, as if she is the other woman. They never tell me these things; I just pay attention and pretend to have stumbled upon them. He's here often I hear, but I never see him and my mama doesn't make him see me and he never asks to see me. After he gets what he came for, he drives back three hours in the opposite direction with pieces of my mama's hopes and dreams in his backseat. I don't know if she believes he isn't seeing other women, but she certainly believes he's not seeing the woman who loves him anymore. This is what he tells her. People believe what they want to believe. She thinks this woman is still in Dallas. I let her believe him. I build Superman back up in the dark.

When this separation begins, I'm extremely young. Young, but old enough to know something ain't quite right when my daddy says *don't be telling yo' mama my business* as he drives me back home after spending a few weeks in Houston. I'm always warned by my mama with things that haven't happened yet like: *don't let him in my house if I ain't there.* I'm always prompted by my daddy with answers to questions I haven't been asked yet, like: *I live by myself.*

I'm young enough to still care if a man is mad at me. I'm young enough to still be afraid of hurting my mama's feelings. I'm still young enough for that now. I keep my mouth closed and pretend I'm not helping to shatter the broken pieces into oblivion. I get really good at being a grown-up like them.

By the second year, the woman who loves my daddy is doing my hair. She puts it in little twists with colorful barrettes that are shaped like bows on top of Christmas presents. She's nice, but when my mama asks, she doesn't exist, but she knows she exists and me not confirming it gives my mama the ok to blame me too.

Year three: Him and her are living together. Sometimes we walk to the corner store and buy pounds of crawfish with spicy potatoes and corn on the cob. My daddy and I don't really have conversations like that. He talks more when she's around. When she's not, I sit in the living room and he stays in the bedroom. He comes out every hour or so to ask me am I ok, am I hungry, am I cold. Gives me a half of watermelon in a pan with salt on it then goes back in his room with the other half. He greets her at the door as if his good day just started.

Year four: The woman who loves my daddy teaches me how to cook some kind of Mexican casserole mixed with beans, ground beef, cheese, and tortillas.

The top layer is made of Jiffy cornbread. It's amazing. She tells me I can't be afraid to get my hands dirty, but to always clean as I go so I won't have a pile of dishes to wash when I finish. I never learned how to clean up the crumbles I leave behind.

Year five: My mama says when I leave for Houston I never call, and when I do, I'm whispering like I have something to hide. I don't want my mama to hear the woman who loves her husband's voice in the background. I tell her that I'll call her back. I never do.

Year six: I'm still young and my mama can't go five minutes without telling me I'm brainwashed—via text and via various confrontations were she assumes I'm lying / have lied about my whereabouts. She's becoming desperate in her darkness when all she has to do is get a divorce. She thinks that by protecting him I am betraying her. But really it's the other way around.

I'm trying to save her from closets.

Year seven: My daddy comes to pick me up for Christmas break. He has his new family in the car outside our door. He parks a couple of houses down and walks to my doorstep like he's taking me to prom. When he knocks on the door, his wife—my mama—answers. She is happy to see him; she is smiling in his face, teasing him, flirting. There's never been a time seeing them intimate has not been weird for me. She tries to walk me out to the car but he doesn't let her. She isn't catching his hints as she keeps pushing forward but I immediately do. I catch the body language. He tries to divert her back into the house, removing her hands from his body; he cannot hurt the woman who loves him. But my mama keeps walking. She gets closer and I get nervous because I know, and I don't want my mama to know that I know. I've been doing so good pretending not to know. We all continue to walk closer and closer to destruction. I watch the horror film in front of me. Something in all of us is about to die. I have my backpack wrapped around my shoulders. I tighten the straps, afraid that I'm leaving for good, scared my mama will not want me back after she finds out, terrified that I failed.

When my mama gets to the passenger side and sees, all she says is *oh, you still messing with her.* This is all she says. This woman who loves her husband doesn't look at my mama. She stares straight ahead. Her too, I assume, realizing my daddy is a backslider, a repeat offender.

My daddy doesn't respond to my mama's statement.

My mama doesn't tell me goodbye.

My daddy just sucks his teeth and runs around to the driver's side.

We leave as quickly as he came.

He drives a car full of women back three hours with an attitude, with a smug frown on his face like we fucked his own shit up. He doesn't talk at all. I try not to cry for all the women inside me and around me the whole ride.

When my mama finally files for divorce, it feels like she not only divorces my daddy, but every once in a while, when the subject is brought up, it feels like she's divorced me too. She looks at me differently, like I'm guilty. Since I was a child, I've never not felt guilty. She hasn't forgiven me so she likes to say things to me that make me cry. It'll come at the most random moments, but they come in swinging. I never said sorry. I later tell her I shouldn't have to. I was a kid even if I had to be their parent. When I'm twenty, when I've still not outgrown her resentment, I say I'm gonna stay in Houston the whole month of July. She texts me:

Wht for . . .
. . . But its nothin i can
Do

When my father quietly remarries after a decade, he doesn't tell me. I find out at a family reunion as the rest of my family congratulates them. He tells me it just seemed like the next step.

One night, after a week of tough encounters between the two of us, we finally have the first of multiple conversations to discuss the past that has never left my present. Like my mama, I work through things over long periods of time. When I tell him the deal, I think I'm 18 or 19 and he is still pretending to be blind as to why his old wife was so stuck on this particular woman. He thinks everything is about him. Says that the reason is he thinks my mama couldn't get over him. I don't tell him she was stuck because of me. That she is stuck because her only child assisted in withholding information. And I quickly realize I am not talking to the man on that recording almost twenty years before. I'm talking to the one who cannot disguise who he is. He tells me he don't know what her problem is because he had plenty of women; this was just the one my mama happened to find out about. He keeps adding on to the list of things I can never tell her. He says this to me with an expression of pride. He laughs this laugh, the same one from that video, except this time this laugh tells me he doesn't really care about women in a way where he can really consider them past what he can take from them. When he tells me about these other, *other,* women, I cannot hold my voice. If I hold my tongue any longer I will swallow it. I will become hoarse. I lick my lips and prepare them to get ready to run through the finish line. I ask him does he really think what he said is funny. I say it with such assurance that he knows what I really mean—I pray in closets to never get stuck with a man like you. I ask him does he love his wife. I hope his answer is completely. She's a way better fit for him, patient and kind and other things the bible says are important. He says she is teaching him how to love. I don't even ask what this means. If he ain't learned by now, why did he waste so many people's time, why did I waste all my energy, why did I lose all my trust for this. He says nobody asked me to do all that.

He doesn't really care. All he cares about is how I am making his new wife feel. He tells me she thinks I don't like her. I think he makes this up just to change the subject. I've done nothing but be respectful and nice to her all these years. If it's been anyone I've been mean to, it's been him. But this is the relationship he would like to mend. I don't ask him the real question: *what about you? do you think what you're doing / what you've done makes me like you?* But I don't know how to say it: I don't think my saying that or this would matter:

I do not believe in marriage.

I do not believe in men.

I do not believe in him.

I cannot forgive him for making me hurt my mama, too.

Whatever I do manage to not say in that moment makes him answer my unasked question. He starts to cry. He says he wishes that I liked him.

I tell him I love him. I hug him with one arm.

My mama has always called me the child of half-truths.

WHEN YOU LEARN THE ALPHABET

Answer the question: In fifth grade, when you were asked to identify your race on the test, why did you circle *other*?

Hint: It wasn't because you didn't know you were/you are, black.

Answer: You circled *other* because you didn't see a box labeled *black,* and you thought maybe the people in charge forgot about your existence. Instead, you saw a box marked *African American.* You didn't know what that meant, so you chose *other* instead.

Other is safe. *Other* can be anything. *Other* cannot hinder you.

You felt good about finally being an other. You weren't too black or too loud on paper. *Other* made you desirable, kinda mysterious. But your mama and daddy made you black, so it's best to love yourself now.

Blood will look thick when you see it melting into a concrete pavement. It looks like the stuff the vampires on *True Blood* drink; thick like corn syrup, but not as sweet because it's leaving a dead boy's body. It's normal now. It's just juice, and he is overflowing into the gutter, spread out like the seasons. His mother will be crying because they are making an example out of her boy. Making an example out of unfulfilled and unnecessary life. The cops on duty will extend this public display of exploitation by saying something like: They can't touch the crime scene

Like: There were no witnesses

They will lie and it will sound like: We will get the person who did this

The news stations and other various forms of media will say something like: He had a criminal record

Like: This is a picture of him

They will mistake his peace sign as a gang sign.

Like: He should have pulled up his pants. He should have listened.

And when you see the dead boy still in the street on your phone screen, they will make sure to zoom in on his big lips just to reiterate the target had been hit. You think, ain't it funny how black people were once mocked for having big, thick, soup-cooling lips, and now the world praises everyone but—for implanting a pair to get a fuller look—and here we are, thick-lipped—and still a tragedy.

Ain't it funny how the lips of that dead boy is now the poster child for sexy.

Church is nonnegotiable. Every Sunday morning you ask why you gotta go, every Sunday. You are there every Wednesday for youth meeting, Thursday for choir rehearsal and some Saturday mornings for holiday program rehearsals. On Sundays, you might not leave. Sunday school is at 9 a.m., morning worship starts at 10:45 a.m., and it's a different kind of Pastor's Anniversary every other week at three o'clock. Your mama says as long as you live in a house where she's paying the bills, you will go wherever she sends you. You say there ain't that much praising the Lord in the world but you will still get dressed and purposely scratch a hole into your stockings—partly because they itch, and mostly to prove a point.

Church will teach you all the books of the bible. Everything will end like Revelation said and you can't wait to see how the locusts will look. But what you'll remember most is Genesis 1:1 when God created the heavens and earth. He made woman out of man. He made flesh out of flesh. Sometimes you scratch your skin and leave pieces of your old self under your fingernails and call it a flesh-eating disease. You will join the children's choir because you have to do something. You can't just sit there. And all the kids in the choir stand will pass Now & Laters back and forth from the same package until there's none left. The old women ushers always have red peppermints in their purses. That's what they give the kids to make them shut up and some Sundays you will settle for them even though you like green peppermints best.

Delivery at your doorstep: a case of strawberry and chocolate milk

Your daddy, the truck-driving milkman for the moment, left it there, left you there.

Eating cereal out of the same bowl for nine straight days gives you time to predict the stamina of material things, time to reflect on clean things. Your mama warned you about eating food that was cooked by unfamiliar hands. You don't know who made it or how their houses look. They might have roaches. They may never wash their hands. You never know. One time this lady made greens and your mama said there were baby roaches inside the pot. Now you only eat your granny's greens, mostly because you're scared of seeing roaches. And Granny's greens taste so good you don't even need the hot sauce.

Fear frightens you.

God gave her power and now her face looks like ripples in the ocean. You know she's gonna die. It's her time to go. She died at ninety-four years old and years before she was gone, her mind made her forget you were born in 1994.

Your great-grandmother used to have all her great-grandchildren on the floor of her yellow wood-paneled house counting out quarters. She had a flower vase full of coins next to her favorite pullout chair and every time ya'll visited, she would spread them out across the floor. A pile in front of each of us. The older you were, the bigger your pile would be. You were the youngest. You have always been the youngest. She'd spread the coins across the rug and tell ya'll to count it out. However much was in your assigned pile, you could keep.

You remember this whenever you remember her. She was giving, she gave. Bowls of Blue Bell Homemade Vanilla. Cans of coke. Lots of coins. You remember death isn't that bad. You knew there'd be days like this and no one had to tell you. You knew how easy it is to forget things sometimes.

Horror story: Your childhood friend goes to jail for not snitching. When his whole life, he's been told a snitch is the worst thing he could be, that there is no safe recovering from it. As a child there were times when ya'll were told to *stop telling all the time.* You stored it just like he did. It was important to determine if you'd be defined by whether or not you were loyal. He was just doing what he was told.

But part of you blames him he's still in a small cell years later for a crime he didn't commit. Part of you blames him for committing to be loyal only. Part of you that follows the impossible expectations of the hood praises him for being some obscured version of a real nigga. Part of you still blames him for falling into the system that was designed specifically for him.

He knows when he returns home, he will be respected.

You know respect is a lot, but it's not everything.

Ignore the idea people actually care what you think. They only care whether or not you think the same way they do.

Journalism was supposed to be your career. You came to college wanting to write about music, wanting to be a critic, because you love to intimidate people with how musically inclined you are. In your Introduction to Journalism class they wanted you to write about news, about politics, about other things you did not care about because politics and news stations do not care about the headline:

8 WARNING SHOTS IN ANOTHER NIGGA'S BACK

Followed by the subheading: *When white people can't disguise their racism any longer*

Journalism doesn't want to talk about that stuff. They'd say you're too close to it, that you have to stick with fact as if the complete disregard of the lives of your cousins uncles friends do not qualify as fact.

Fact 1. They can, but won't, print a headline with the n-word in it. They will say you can't say that word, it's offensive. But when they say it's offensive, what they really mean is they're just upset they can't say it, publically anyways, and especially in a headline.

Fact 2. If you had stuck with fact, the headline would've read instead:

> WHY IS IT OKAY FOR YOU TO CALL ME A NIGGA IN THE PRIVACY OF YOUR HOME BUT I'M NOT ALLOWED TO SAY MY OWN NAME
>
> Followed by a longer subheading that's not really a subheading:

Black people were offended when you allowed us to breastfeed your children but wouldn't let us use the same bathroom in fear of catching nigga diseases. Black people were offended when ya'll blamed rap music for a fraternity's racist chant. Black people live in offense.

Followed by a shorter subheading:

So niggas freely using the word nigga is just something ya'll gone have to deal with.

But they would just tell you a subheading can't be that long.

Kinetic energy flows through the nigga veins apparently. They can jump higher, dance better, dunk a ball with style, prophesize from prison, make a crowd laugh, throw a punch harder, be a human auction, write a rap song eloquently, have their hair stand tall, be target practice, throw a football, pick cotton in a hot field, play an instrument seductively, start a riot while trying to start a revolution. And, if it's absolutely necessary, they can even outrun a fat ass cop, because you know they're on their second strike and ain't tryna get locked back up. You know they're good at going to prison.

Lying to God may be illegal, you're not sure, but sometimes you do it just in case you run out of mercy. Forgive me. I'm sorry. I won't do it again.

A priest lying to you is still legal across countries though.

Money will always be an issue. You don't love money and everyone around you is in a by-any-means-necessary sacrificial relationship to get it. They love the idea of money more than they love themselves. No one in your family has money enough to where they don't have to worry about money. Spending their checks on cash cars and weed. When the money runs low, they just sell their food stamps for half-price and call it a day.

Next semester's tuition will be going up by only .3%. *Only .3%.* They think you should be grateful of this.

Bria says you should strip; you can cover that .3% in one night. You tell her your ass isn't big enough. She tells you to start squatting and eventually it will round out. You tell her you bend over backward for enough people already.

Oppression will come mostly in darker hues. And you know the world is not black and white, but that's just because no one wants to admit it is. Your daddy will tell you no matter how much you are aware of white people issues, about the drugs they use, about the lives they live, they don't give a damn about the black ones. He will say they don't give a fuck about us in the most disrespectful way he can. It'll have the time his boss called him a nigger inside his throat when he says it. He choked him out. You can hear he's still mad about that one. You can also hear he's still proud about that one. You will be proud of him. He says they don't care about relating *to* you, they care only about creating *from* you. And you'll sit on the couch and stare at all three of your white roommates and say to yourself they've never even asked what the real issue was as you watched the Ferguson "riots" on bullshit CNN because they'd rather be watching *How I Met Your Mother*. Because you will remember when P said there is nothing anyone could say or do to him that can make him feel bad about being white.

Psychology says everything you do has meaning behind it and you watched yourself attempt to victimize your decisions and behaviors and personality.

Your aunt was yelling *I HOPE YOU OD ON THE MEDICINE!!! I HOPE YOU OD ON THE MEDICINE!!!* Because she acts crazy when she hasn't swallowed a couple of pills. She also acts crazy when she has. The doctor told her she's bipolar, has OCD, and Tourette's syndrome. When she told you this you laughed and so did she. She will get three checks every month and she will accept whatever they say is wrong with her. She tells people this diagnosis, but she forgets to add a man beat her every day just for being pretty, which will be why she likes to fight. Forget to say she won't sit still because she has drugs in her system that is working and eating at her cells. Her teeth will chatter because she hasn't had enough money for a hit in about a week so she'll lash out at anyone who isn't fighting a twenty-year addiction.

You pray for her, because prayer hands are stronger than weighted ones.

Quiet rooms are the ones holding all the family secrets. Places like funerals, and weddings, and grandparent's houses.

At the funeral your mama said Grandmother was mean and prejudice and had favorites.

At your grandparent's house, no one talks about why certain people can't get along and who is actual family by blood, but food is always around to keep you quiet.

Repeat the phrase: *lead us not into temptation but deliver us from evil*

Everything you know about the bible, your mother told you. When you try to read for yourself, you get really drowsy.

Sixteen candles—you've completed childhood so you take one trip to Wal-Mart. When you turned sixteen you asked for a purity ring. You don't know why you didn't think to go to a bible store or somewhere that specializes in cleansing the body because all the jewelry stores in the mall said they weren't sure if they sold purity rings. But they do have rings you could buy and just default as a purity ring. Like a backup plan ring. Like a plan b ring. They will say it's a good thing to see such a young girl wanting one though. You'll say thanks and settle for a ring with two hearts intertwined together, one pink, one silver.

Your purity was worth only one hundred dollars. It has to be worth pennies by now.

Two is not better than one and you have a problem with greedy people.

You're nineteen with two jobs and a full-time academic schedule. At your morning job they rake in over one million dollars black Friday weekend and you work those mornings mourning, dragging your feet with a $7,000 balance still in your student account. You work the cash register and the people you work with actually care about this job. You can't physically handle the idea of being passionate about being a Best Buy employee. At nineteen this is a good job. You get benefits 'nshit. It's a good job, if you don't mind those walkie-talkies tracking your every move. It's a good job if you don't mind spending hours taking online tests that determine whether you're gifted and talented enough to call the credit card company when a customer's card gets declined. It's a good job if you don't mind that same customer cussing your ass out. It's a good job if you don't mind you work at an electronics store but are using the first computer ever made for checkouts and the screen freezes regularly. It's a good job if you've been there for two months and don't mind one of the managers physically moving you out of the way because he's trying to impress a pretty lady at your register and you're moving too slowly and making him look incompetent. It's only a good job if you plan on staying there.

Your night job is around the corner so you walk there in two minutes to start your second shift. This job won't let you paint your nails red or any other color because it might chip into a customer's corned beef sandwich. And if it wasn't for the customer who asked you were you deaf because you couldn't input his sandwich order as swiftly as he recited it in all of three breaths, you'd understand. What you don't understand is why your register is always short when this particular manager is closing. One time $75 short.

After you counted out your register and brought him the receipt, you just stared at him for a long time. He understood your face. He said he'd figure it out just like you knew he would.

You go back home for Christmas break with both of your jobs awaiting your return. While you're there, you watch an interview your favorite rapper gave on capitalism. He said we as a people are accepting our lives are only worth twelve dollars an hour. You get paid nine fifty. He said we on a plantation, making someone else richer while we still struggle to put food on the table every night. But we gotta eat, only if it's a little bit, so we stay on this plantation for all of our lives.

It takes seconds for you to decide when you go back to school, you won't be going back to work. And you don't care to call and say that you quit. And you don't care to go pick up your last check. But you know it was only $163 because they gave you minimum hours.

Understand telling a lie is the same as murder is the same as rape is the same as adultery. You're a liar. You lie, you'll steal. You steal, you'll kill. That's how this sinning thing works.

Until you got caught in a big lie, you didn't care how much you did it. You'd lie just to end a conversation. You'd lie so you could hear the TV again. You'd lie, and then someone would lie to you and somehow their lie was more potent. But you know no sin is greater than the other.

So you have been practicing truth-telling, they say in twenty-eight days it will become a habit. The truth is: black lives do not matter to a large percent of our population, and you wish they would stop lying for ratings, ignorance ain't bliss, violence isn't the answer, but . . . it gets shit done from time to time, and Clinton had sexual relations with that woman.

You go Bill.

"Virginity isn't real," your roommate says, "because your hymen grows back after you haven't had sex in a while. Maybe a couple of months—*it . . . grows . . . back.*"

You want so badly to ask has her hymen grown back and has she ever met anyone whose hymen has grown back because if she has, there is a bigger issue that needs to be discussed. Everyone in the room agrees with her. You want so badly to ask if your hymen grows back, how long does it take.

You don't know at the time, she is both right about one thing and very, very, wrong about the other.

Withdrawal from people who look like you is a real thing. Your school is predominately—and systematically—white. And one time you had to go over to K's room just to be around some familiarity. It felt kind of hypocritical because you came to this school not wanting to go to a historically black college and now you think about this decision a lot. That you thought too many black people wouldn't help you grow because you've spent your entire life around too many black people, and now you're in a place where you barely see them.

Now you answer questions about weaves. You say they come in *12"*
14"
16"
18"
up to however many inches you want.

You answer questions asking whether or not you've personally been treated wrong by a white person. You answer questions about how much seasoning you put on your food. About your afro when you take your weave out. About lotion. About perms. About everything you wouldn't have to answer if you went to a black college.

You say it is ok to ask. You just mind you are solely looked upon to represent an entire race. You mind white people can represent themselves, but what they think of you specifically, will be what they believe your entire race is like. Their questions sound like *you people.* You mind you have to give the correct answer, not your answer. You mind you have to be a collective voice. You hope they shiver when you speak.

X is the number of people who can embody selflessness: you do not know these people.

Yesterday you called your dad. He asked how you were doing. You said you were fine. He asked how is school. You said you're not gonna get all A's this semester. He said you just have to work harder next semester. *The phone gets static on the line because no one is speaking.*

You ask him what is he doing. He says he's watching the game. You ask who's playing. He says the Rockets. You say they're going to lose. He says they beat the sorry Mavericks. You say barely. *The phone gets static on the line because no one is speaking.*

He asks do you want to watch the game with him. You ask what channel is it on. He says channel 45. You go into your living room and turn on the TV. He asks are you watching. You say yea. *The phone gets static on the line because no one is speaking.*

Zigzag is the pattern you have to run in if a snake is chasing you.

You are still running in circles.

FATHER CAN YOU HEAR ME

Our men our daddies and the man we cannot keep are all the same person.

Our daddies ran away at birth—as if they never existed.
To the outside world we look like Immaculate Conception.
It's as if we just appear in throngs to become the world's greatest
at something.
As if we do not have an origin story.

We are magnificent in ways we don't always have fathers, yet almost always we look exactly like our disappearing daddies.

They went away on drug binges / to Houston / some were stolen from us / they do not marry our mothers / some just go, we do not know where to / to jail / to hell, possibly. Some just didn't care enough to get away; they are in the same cities as us—my granddaddy lived 45 minutes away from my mama, her two sisters, and their brother until the day he died.

We all, the aftermath / the children, automatically connect with our runaways by blood. There are attitudes and eyes and everything else our mamas romanticized about them in our faces, in our bodies. We just forget mama don't love these things no more and no amount of soap can wash their imprints off us. We can't scrub off the lies and make our mamas feel better. We do not know what our real faces look like. We do not know the actuality of anything.

My daddy apologized to me once during Ludacris's episode of *Behind the Music*. Ludacris was describing the feeling he felt when his daughter was born. He was explaining a necessity he had to always be in her life.

The lights in the room dimmed some.
He was explaining a common theory of what it means to be a real man.
The lights in the room dimmed some more.
He was verbalizing love.
The lights in the room dimmed some more.
He was explaining how he loved his child more than he loved being right.
Then the room we were in became dark.
My daddy said: I'm sorry I wasn't there like I probably shoulda been

* *

He probably was right
I probably shoulda said: I forgive you

There isn't one way to go about parenting us. Our traditions are a little bit different. A lot of us were raised under the open hand of a woman of some sort, a grandmother / a mama / an aunt, it really does take a village / women who, just like us, did not have steady men in their lives, so they tried to fill those empty spaces with cornbread and cabbage.

They did not know what else to feed us.

The unsaid rule is: we laugh and play around about our missing parent, but no one else can. There are reoccurring jokes about our nonexistent, sometimes rocky, relationships with our daddies and how they leave / when they leave / why they never fully return

Like: him going to the store and never coming back

Like: playing catch in the yard with an invisible man

Like: imagining conversations

Like: never attending a daddy/daughter dance

Like: him saying he will pick you up for the weekend and you are overflowing out of your socks with joy that you wait for him all night until you finally fall asleep on the couch. Funny, only when they are coming out of the mouth of someone who can relate, because these happenings, more times than not, are too true. The kind of truth that makes you laugh with a pang of misplaced comfort. It's too real to not know how to properly communicate. It's too real to be afraid to talk to your mama about him. It's too real for some of us to not even know what he looks like.

For some little girls and boys, we meet our daddies for the first time deep inside our adult lives. In these cases, maybe a child of our own or a series of unanswered questions about why we behave in the manner we do will trigger us to reach out. We think we are missing something important. We need to know why we were left with a bunch of women who could not teach us balanced love.

This one thing is certain for all absentee daddies. I have not witnessed one to prove me wrong and I badly wish for one to do so. When you finally talk face to face, you will go through a process of disbelief, a wave of rock bottom sadness, and an ultimate high of disgust.

Your daddy, whom you haven't laid eyes on in over a decade. Your daddy, who you see once a year and finally summoned up the courage to question. Your daddy, who you are exactly like, will say to you in one way or another

a. it was your mother who kept him away (not in a literal sense but in ways that attacked his ego)
b. he could not financially provide for you (he thinks that is his sole purpose for your life)
c. the past is in the past (meaning he is afraid of you and what you will say to him so he just wants you to forget it. he is saying do not hold him accountable for something that has already happened, but he is not saying things will change)
d. he isn't completely at fault; he cannot and will not take the full blame, that you, the child, could have reached out too

To him, who knows nothing about you except you may, or may not, carry his last name, will always believe the phone works both ways

I guess he wants you to be his father too

There is an episode of *The Fresh Prince of Bel-Air* I hate to love called "Papa's Got a Brand New Excuse." In this episode Will's distant daddy decides to show up. He sells his son dreams of a father/son connection and Will is happy.

We, the audience / the kids who are just like Will, are happy he got his father back, too.

At the end of the episode when Will's daddy is preparing to leave without a goodbye and inevitably letting his child down for what feels like the last time, Will is yelling he doesn't need him because he learned how to drive / how to shave / how to fight without him and confessing how he endured fourteen birthdays without him and never even received as much as a birthday card, he cries out TO HELL WITH HIM!!!!

and we, the audience / the kids who are just like Will,
have memorized this scene verbatim, and I, try not to tear up every time it airs. We all share a subliminal silent group hug every time we see Will ask,

how come he don't want me man?

I try to internalize whether there are distinct differences between fatherless boys and girls, whether one is affected more severely, whether either are affected at all. And all I can come up with is what we have in common. We both know of a man who strikingly resembles what we perceive to be all of our flaws. We only acknowledge them when we want to feel sorry for ourselves, when we need someone to take the fall. We only acknowledge them for the bad and never the trial and error. We never acknowledge that them not being around could potentially be the thing that saved us from being sadder.

The similarities between us are we're both affected to our disadvantage. We don't have the privilege of seeing consistent men in our vicinities. Faithful men. Godly men. It's not often we get to see black men taking care of black women and children, loving black women and children, protecting black women and children, or even loving other black men for that matter, or raising black families. Loving their daughters, molding their sons on a day-to-day basis. Instead we turn into weekend babies / summer children / phone call kids.

I mean, we are already black; we cannot afford to be bastards too.

We need to be engaged in the actual lives of men. Not Michael Kyle from *My Wife & Kids,* not Furious Styles in *Boyz n the Hood,* not Julius from *Everybody Hates Chris,* not Randall Pearson from *This Is Us,* or John Quincy Archibald in *John Q*—men who are giving us complex ideas of what a good father is so heavily that we start to believe they're real. Men who—although honorable and instill a sense of pride in us—cannot have a realistic impact on our lives. We need to see men in our families, in our homes, with loud personalities and a firm sense of self, we need to see them make mistakes and fix them. We need to know they are there. We need to know you are here.

When I was younger I used to take satisfaction in saying not having a serious father did not affect how I'm continuously turning out. I took satisfaction in not needing him, minimal interaction became enough because I didn't want to be let down. I didn't even try to entertain the practicalities of it all. I was good. Until I finally understood I could not modify my daddy's awareness, I began to forgive him in small doses. I'm still forgiving him in small doses. I know his guilt may be something that will always be stronger than his presence. I know his pride has always rubbed off on me.

Sometimes when we talk, there is a disconnect between him and his pain, between him and his responsibility. A disconnect between him and his truth. I hear about a similar pain in hip-hop / in poetry / in my daddy's throat when he's tryna hold in the truth instead of saying it aloud.

It is to be said, and not to be excused, that a lot of daddies are living in fear of recreating their own fatherless childhoods.

Jay-Z, for instance, wrote a song about the joys of new fatherhood when his first daughter was first born called "Glory." It even had her happy voice in the background as theme music. And then soon after, Jay-Z wrote a song about his realities when fatherhood presented itself to him without a mask to cover it up.

In "Jay-Z Blue" from his highly underrated 2013 album *Magna Carta Holy Grail,* Jay interprets his own fatherless childhood and how it could so easily happen to his seed without preparation or warning. He says things

Like: *Please don't judge me, only hugged the block, I thought my daddy didn't love me*

Like: *I don't wanna duplicate it. I seen my mom and pop drive each other mothafuckin crazy and I got that nigga blood in me. I got his ego and his temper; all I'm missing is the drugs in me*

Like: *Father never taught me how to be a father, treat a mother*

Like: *I don't wanna have to just repeat another, leave another, baby with no daddy, don't want no mama drama*

This sensation doesn't vary much. My daddy had a providing father in his presence every day but that doesn't mean he had a man to model after. In fewer words, he has communicated to me the same terrors of this song. So has my cousin who has a daughter. So has my uncle who has a son. They all consume the same hurts. Yet how these men go about being fathers all clash with one another—all crash into their offspring—all crumble into us writing about it twenty years later.

For some unknown reason after my daddy says something to me he wishes he didn't, he asks nicely am I mad. I can depend on him to be worried if I hate him or not. I always say no. He says he doesn't mean to be nasty. I repeat: I'm not mad. I don't get angry anymore. I'm aware of what he's capable of giving, and I expect nothing more than what he's gonna give. I just have to be willing to give something back.

Growing up, this is what I comprehended about men. They were beautiful too black and too strong, they were too majestic for this world. They walked to a rhythm. Their skin was golden, no matter the shade, like trophies, and their voices sounded like the bass in my trunk. I knew I wanted one since I was a child.

Something about them read as the standard; no matter how many bad encounters I've had with one. This is what I thought / what I think. I just didn't have anything in my personal life to compare my vision to. There was no way I could have them for an extended period of time; they were not mine to keep, they do not like confinement / obligation / dependency. They are too hard and unwilling to break.

In Kiese Laymon's book of essays *How to Slowly Kill Yourselves and Others in America,* he hints at fatherhood and the idea of kids needing more than just fathers in their life to fully survive. He says, "Black children need waves of present, multifaceted love, not simply present fathers." This is true and I agree, we need multiple forces of outside love, but I also believe we need love in the home to know how to receive love secondarily. His notion of love being synonymous with survival, a carnal need, is a technique fatherless children cannot comprehend, for we cannot take love.

We fuck love up.

Our backstories ain't that different.

Girls need fathers for this very reason. We need fathers to avoid looking for one in boys most importantly / so we won't be afraid of men / so we can know how a man is supposed to treat us / so we don't think we need a man to be able to be a woman / so we learn how to take direction / so we won't mature into adult girls with distrustful hearts.

Boys need fathers so they won't grow into adult boys who think women owe them something / so they won't grow up to say they only date white girls because we're too difficult / so they won't grow up thinking they have to suppress any emotion that isn't attached to a temper tantrum / black boys need black fathers so they won't turn into another statistic.

We need multifaceted love but we also need simple, unconditional love so when we find someone to love on our own, it doesn't become hard to decipher whether we are sorting out our daddy issues or if it is a tangible, lasting thing.

My daddy told me once the women in my family cannot keep a man / we run them off / we are too attached to the women in our family opposed to the men we entertain. He remembers my family as a bad experience. I do not know how to separate his experience with my family and his experience with me.

In Laymon's book, he also said he isn't the only boy who realized a long time ago that his mother and her mother and her mother's mother "needed loving, generous partners far more than [black boys] needed present fathers"—my mama does not understand this, she is too hard and unwilling to break. She isn't too strong to believe she needed help, but she is too strong to ask for it.

My mother never remarried after my daddy showed himself to be no different than her father. / My Granny never remarried after marrying an older, fatherlike figure. / My great-grandmother had two divorces. I don't really know any of the men.

A genuine trust of the opposite sex is a distance hard to travel. Our peaks become a midpoint. A place where things are just getting started. We leave first.

We never speak to the boys we like or the men we could have loved again. It is not that we can't keep a man, it's that we never learned how to be kept, and I still don't know whether this is something that can be reversed, or if I even want to reverse it.

My daddy apologized to me once on a ride to Popeye's. He dropped me off and said to not take his tone so literally.

When they leave, what I think they're saying is
let me go
don't nothing grow here
Like: me
Like: me
Like: me
/ like you / like simple sentences / like roots that have not been watered

THE BITCH HAD DISCIPLINE

When I first met Amy Elliot Dunne in Gillian Flynn's extremely long-winded 2012 novel *Gone Girl*, my initial thought was, this bitch is crazy. Intuitively and exclusively crazy. The kidnapping. The murder. The chase. The commitment to the plan. The improvisation within the missteps. I had seen white women ruin lives many times but I never seen them follow through on their own merit, and without an accomplice to do the dirty work the way Amy did. It was wild to read at the time, but the sensational aspect of Amy's personality still wasn't enough to strip me from the moments that required me to admit a part of me kinda liked the woman. The bitch had discipline, and many other quality strengths I admire and hope to someday emulate without force. She had enormous drive. She had vision. She executed her vision past her wildest expectations.

After her plan to annihilate her husband's entire existence was put into motion, she delivers this monologue on the theory of Cool Girls, something the plot of the book combats to no end. It goes: "Men always say that as the defining compliment, don't they? She's a Cool Girl. Being the Cool Girl means I am a hot, brilliant, funny woman who adores football, poker, dirty jokes, and burping, who plays video games, drinks cheap beer, loves threesomes and anal sex, and jams hot dogs and hamburgers into her mouth like she's hosting the world's biggest culinary gang bang while somehow maintaining a size 2, because Cool Girls are above all hot. Hot and understanding. Cool Girls never get angry; they only smile in a chagrined, loving manner and let their men do whatever they want. Go ahead, shit on me, I don't mind, I'm the

Cool Girl. Men actually think this girl exists. Maybe they're fooled because so many women are willing to pretend to be this girl."

Throughout most of my life, I had always been the Coolest Girl in the world to some male peer. Cool had become my name, my definitive characteristic, my eventual character flaw. Some part of me has always gravitated toward the interests of the boys around me, whether it be my taste in music, which has always placed me high on the cool scale, or maybe it was my half-assed attempts at putting together an outfit, or because I'm funny to a certain extent, or that I'm able to keep up with the banter and can take a joke without getting sensitive because that's what I've been conditioned to do so boys will like me. All these things deemed me the girl who got it, who understood the holistically gendered dependency it took to keep up. I used these attributes to my advantage in ways that never possessed tangible advantages—meaning—I did all this work to separate myself from the women they talked about in a negative tone. I didn't wanna be labeled any harsh words. So I found myself being just like the boys who wanted to be just like other boys arguably more fucked up than them. It was weird how easily I could conform. Like them, I used to wanna be like my favorite rappers spending thousands of dollars on women then letting them go. I used to wanna fuck and not care after. I wanted to be like these men instead of who I was. I wanted to be like these men instead of my favorite black women who were hurting because nobody loved them back. I didn't wanna feel that hopeless. I blocked them out. I didn't wanna face myself, who I could be. The boys saw these things I was trying to accomplish as reflections of them, and of course, they thought their reflections were something to aspire to, so how could they blame me. I was feeding their ego. Coddling their pride. I don't know anything about being a man, and the cooler I got, with my sneaker collection and my fake confidence, I only found myself knowing what it's like—even with all these things—to still be the axis that he revolves on. Because even cool girls can't get away from cool boys who gets off by hearing their own voices knowing damn well they aren't really saying anything. And that shit is played out.

I think this is why Amy intrigued me so much. She was who—in some less violent ways—I was fighting to become in the presence of men. Although I can't exactly follow the exact blueprint, because the consequences of faking my own death/kidnapping, sending my entire town on a scavenger hunt for my missing body, committing a senseless murder for my own personal agenda, and coming back home to a clean slate only to make demands that will be met without question all because I cried the same way she did and actually have people believe me are slim to none. I know her crazy will be dismissed for victimhood, her crazy will be clinical, mine would be defined as identity. I saw this clearly, I always see this clearly, but I also saw that at the root of her decisions—the fake death, the real murder, the master plan—was a great deal of self-love. Her manic actions, although very brave, isn't the reason she intrigues me. I'm intrigued by the way she stopped caring about men's feelings. She couldn't care less about what you would feel, as long as she was felt. She didn't let being seen in a particular way stop her from being who she wanted to be. She wasn't afraid to be too much of something. She was overabundant. Excessive. Overwhelming. Full. Greedy. For she was just another woman—on a never-ending list of women—who felt stupid for allowing herself to play small to a man she knew she was better than, smarter than, stronger than. She was just another woman—on a never-ending list of women—who felt stupid for allowing a man to let her forget who the fuck she was for the sake of who he thinks he is. The book showcased her outgrowing her mental conditioning. She became a woman who told and stopped asking, and this—she knew—automatically eliminates you from being a cool girl. And I know that if you're afraid to disagree with men, then it's kind of hard to be in agreement with women when you should. That's the unfair trade in being any girl, not just a cool one. And feeling that pang of *not you too,* when men feel you have turned against them, like they are tired and tired and why can't they just find one woman who doesn't expect them to be decent to other women as long as they are decent to you, hurts when you are trying to be the cool girl, but feels like pure comedy when you stop caring. The older I grew, I saw myself becoming less and less cool to men than I'd ever been. And at this point in my life, I'd much rather be any other girl, the normal girl, the plain girl, the mean girl, the weird girl, than the cool one.

My father, born of apparent aloofness, various phobias, and privilege he refuses to acknowledge, calls me a feminist. It comes out of his mouth like disappointment. Like: *you one of them feminist bitches who ain't never satisfied huh?* And it honestly, truly, brings a smile to my face. To describe me to myself, he uses words like extremist / sneaky / chauvinist / man-hater, and this is all in one sitting. He says, *I ain't never heard you agree with a man.* Which just means he ain't never heard me agree with him. He—like most men who are apprehensive about a woman who knows what she's talking about—like to say these kinds of things, these kinds of words, when you challenge anything in simple conversation. They think the negative connotations attached to them will make you shut up. But these words, in all of my adult life, have never scared me. I probably am too extreme sometimes, I'm most definitely a feminist, and I'm probably a man-hater too depending on the man in question. This doesn't make me feel like less of anything really. It fuels me, gives me strength. I figure if men don't have anything nice to say about me once I finally close my mouth, I'm on the right side of history, or at least in the midst of a constantly moving current.

You would think if women can survive everything we go through in a man's world—everything we are called—the never-ending violences our bodies are expected to accept and overlook—everything we are diluted to—everyone else's weight we are expected to carry—and everything we are seen as through man's eyes on an hour-to-hour basis without much relief—niggas would be feminists too. But no. Instead, they make you the angry, bitter, black bitch who can't get no man then have the audacity to ask who hurt you. And it takes a fist down my throat to not say, Bitch. You did.

At the very least, you would think they would be able to handle something as minute as **MEN ARE TRASH** every now and then, but no, they get deep in their feelings. They're quick to isolate themselves. Say it's not all men. But once upon a time, the late, great one they call Tupac asked a very relevant question when speaking about the derogatory terms he chooses to use to describe women in his music, "If you not a bitch then why the fuck are you in that conversation?"

So, if you personally aren't trash . . . why the fuck are you in the conversation? Who hurt you? What will it take to stop your pain before I stop my own? How can I pacify you today sir?

I never had issues with men until I kept having issues with men. And the older I got the more those issues grew for me. I have a problem with men trying to tell me what to do. A problem with control. A problem with letting control go in the presence of men. A problem with men. I am stiff. Defensive. I don't like to hear direction or advice in their voices, it makes me nervous. I'm jealous of the way they can direct instructions to me expecting their needs to be met like *baby girl, i know you can do it on your own, but let me show you how to do it* ***right***. I can't handle the superiority that is oozed out of every syllable, the entitlement in how they speak to women, the fear they place in them. I'm disgusted at how we dismiss this all by letting men be men. Directly or indirectly, I find myself struggling with gifting empathy their way. Most times I just do not care what the fuck they are complaining about. If I never have to hear a man complaining about baby mamas and the price of government issued child support that's BASED ON YOUR INCOME ever again, it would be too soon. I have a hard time giving men credit for being better, for being different. It's as if they crave credit for doing what they're supposed to be doing. They want me to say thanks for being honest. Thanks for treating me like a person. Thanks for taking care of their own children. I'm not saying thank you for nothing. It's a mental barrier I've been trying to work through, but it's as if when they speak, my natural reaction is to combat what they say whether right or wrong. My natural reaction is to disagree, to say no. To rebut. To rebel. To free myself from their strong hold on my free speech.

I know men I should love but I don't and maybe that makes me a bad person. I forget they love love too. They need love too. And I don't think the way I'm set up stores enough of it. Which is probably why I've never had a close male relationship where I felt I could lose control, be myself, and still be safe. Not with my father, not with any uncle, not with any friend, cousin, grandparent, or teacher. I've always felt as if myself would be too much for them. That I wouldn't know what to do with my whole self. They wouldn't know what to do with it. That they'd want to give it back. It would be too disruptive, too loud, too confrontational, too feminine, too hard. That they would give it back after I let it loose because they've always gotten their way; they're spoiled by birth. That I wouldn't know how to put it back once it was loose. I've learned how to be a small fraction of a woman through watching men. I see myself reflected in them. Just like them, everything about me either grows too fast or not at all. The parts of myself I know hurt people. The parts I know are capable. The part of myself that shuts down after one disappointment. The parts that know I can be just like them if I really wanted to and not feel bad about it. They teach me everything I know about contradiction. I think of men I love, both my senior and my junior. How we are suns set ablaze. No matter how cool we get, we can never get by on our chemistry for too long. We merge—then burn out—then clash into dominion. I see them and I see me at the same time in the dust, terrified of who I might become or if I already became it.

I'm not against men, and I think it's stupid that I even have to say that. I love men. I fall in fake love with one every single day and I'm not even exaggerating. The way they move. The way the skin around their jaw line looks vacuum-sealed. Their hands. Their fingers. The fingers Lord. The bottomless hues of their complexions. The subtle wilt of their eyelids when they laugh too hard. These hard-to-find but very natural attributes, I love them all. I actually have discussions with women all the time about what we love about men more than we discuss what we don't. But one thing I've noticed is it always comes down to a list of attributes, these physical contributions. Always. My best friend and mama both tell me at the top of their list of things they love about men, a penis takes the cake. I laugh. I think, all this time I've been worried about men not liking women as human beings yet compensating by being deeply in love with pussy, when maybe women don't really like men either. We like things that are extensions of them—that are ideas of them—that are dreams of what their potential could lead to, when they are doing the absolute bare minimum in the flesh in order to bring that potential to fruition. So we cling to these attributes, and require nothing more, lose our discipline, our focus, our knees, instead of making them be accountable in the ways in which they need to do better, instead of being accountable for how we too need to do better.

I care about them. Where they're going, how they'll get there, how they're feeling in their bodies. I mean, they are dying after all. I process men differently in different mirrors. I know there are those who love me back. I just wished men I have been born of listened when women—when I—have screamed stop. Instead of pretending we weren't as urgent because he is the only one allowed to have problems. I wish men I have been born of understood I am a black woman in America, under him. With issues outside of him. With issues that stem directly from him. Because unlike everyone else around me who doesn't look like me, I am not granted the privilege of being mediocre.

I think about Amy Elliot Dunne a lot, for showing me that an unpleasant bitch accomplishes way more shit than a cool one. How easily she could now roam around without the expectation of being a good woman on her back. How free she must have felt when she captured her control back, when she was on fire rummaging through the things she left behind. How she didn't have to suppress herself anymore. How forgetting how to say sorry for things she really meant was one of her greatest accomplishments. How being a man is kinda fun.

LEGS ON HIS SHOULDERS

He says,
if he's going to take this seriously,
right now you're too independent; it's unattractive.
He needs to feel needed more.

He says, his woman is an extension of him.
He says, don't be an embarrassment.

He says, you need to start thinking for yourself
when he is not there to think for you. That you
need to prove to him he made the right choice in choosing you.

He says, you need to cover
up more when people are around, stop parading
what is his, and where do you think you're going
with that dress on, smell good
cook regularly, listen, be pretty without
makeup,
he likes the natural look more.

He says, you can leave, but there is no one else
who can make you feel the way he can make
you feel, he
makes you feel good makes you **feel**, *feel*
something about yourself, makes you feel, makes you moan
makes you cry makes you laugh makes you sing
in the shower

makes you feel so good, he says *baby have you ever felt this good*

too scared to say baby you make me feel like nothing,

He says, you don't understand
what it means to be a man—to be strong
without reason. All the pressure on his
shoulders. The pressure of your legs around
his shoulders, it's becoming too much. The
pressure of your hands pressing down on his
shoulders—he says, you ask for too much.
He says, you are just making it worse. He
says, this is a woman's problem; she doesn't
know when to shut up.

He says, you don't get to question a
grown ass man
about his decisions
even if they affect
you.

He says, these feminist bitches are getting out of hand.
Want too much but do too little. What about what men want.

He says, it's so ***simple***—the male brain, why can't you grasp it. Why can't you anticipate his needs.

He says, what he has is his and what you have is his, too.
Says you should be thanking him for the things
He lit inside your body.

Thanking him and thanking him and
thanking him for everything and thanking him, thank you
he says you should learn to say thank you, don't you know

how many women are willing to lick his wounds only for him
to make brand new ones on their skin.
He says, he lies out of love for you.
He says, your daddy must have really fucked you up.

He says more and more until his tongue is bleeding.
Natural disasters are occurring globally, there is an act of God
brewing in his ribcage:
He asks why do you always want to argue.

He says stay in your place.
He says, do you really think someone
else will treat
you better.

He says, you think you're
better than him,
Like, nothing matters
Like, he doesn't matter

He says, it's hard to say no to all of them.
He shifts. He means, take what you can get because not many
men would
put up with your attitude the way he does.

He says, you ain't all that.
He says, he picked up trash on the side of the
road before and
made it pretty—turned it ugly—dropped it
back off on a
backstreet—made sure no one
would want it anymore.
He says, you go looking for something you gone
find it.

He says,
what you won't do another
girl will.

He says, if you leave him, don't come back because he'll be
gone. He's never not been heard.

He says, he knew you were no different.
He says, what kind of woman doesn't stick it out when things get rough.

He says, women ain't supposed to act like this, all removed.
He says, why can't you ever be there for him.

He says, you can't give up on him now, if you just give
him
a little more time he could be ready. If you could just
sit back and
wait
a little bit longer.
If you could just give him and give him until he is ready
to give
back. That is what a good woman does,

he says,

it's cool, women bow down to him every day.
Lie down on
their backs and he spreads his burdens out on
top of them.
Covers them like cloth. Melt into their bloodstream
like a poison,
their legs on his shoulders. It's too bad, he says, that
you gave up.
never wrapped your hands around your
own throat.
never let him get away with trying.

FOR SALE, SOMETIMES FOR FREE

In 1998—when I was four—my parents took me to the movie theater to see Ice Cube's directorial debut, *The Player's Club*, a film about a college student who—in order to continue her education—turns to stripping to pay her tuition. In 1998, the stigma that came with dancing for dollars was that the act is immoral. Provocative. Scandalous. A hoe activity. Stripping had not yet branded itself into an athletic career, into a semi–art form, into an extension of dance and movement. In 1998, stripping was still just another avenue to shame women and justify it by saying they're the ones disgracing themselves.

In *The Player's Club*, the film's protagonist Diana—stage name "Diamond"—is understandably anxious and nervous the first time she gets on stage, even though she's capable of fulfilling her job's requirements. The scene's build up is expected seeing as how its an extension of her good girl gone undercover storyline. She covers her body with her hands as her stiff hips sway to the seductive music. As the movie progresses, the audience can see Diamond become more comfortable in her nakedness, in her persona. We see the hands fall and we bare witness to the bodily reveal that indicates her commitment to the fast money. But after a run-in with a couple of coworkers, she quickly learns the political and hypocritical ins and outs of the nightlife, which causes her to choose to separate her professional and personal lives. She learns that being displayed onstage is just her job, just a means of survival, and to *make the money, don't let the money make you.*

Diamond is in direct juxtaposition to Ebony—her cousin—who later enters the club scene, only to become consumed with the thrill of possibility. Ebony's journey reveals itself in all the stereotypical, live fast burn out strife. Even though they share the same job, Ebony and Diamond's perceptions of their experiences couldn't be any more different. From the beginning, Diamond is seen as the one who can be saved. Ebony, on the other hand, is the one who's left to be consumed and abandoned.

The Player's Club isn't scarce in sex, nudity, sexual violence, or sensuality at the expense of a black woman's body. Sometimes it's uncomfortable to watch how easily the common decency humanity should provide their bodies is erased. So it's safe to say when I first saw the movie, I mostly listened to it and I watched portions of it peeking through my mama's fingers.

Two years later—when I'm six—my mama and I are walking down the street when she asks me do I know what sex is. I do. By this time, I've watched enough TV, listened to enough Prince albums, and eavesdropped on enough adult conversations to figure it out. When adults spelled out S-E-X as if it wasn't a one syllable, three-letter word, I would store it in my memory. I knew sex was way more than babies. I knew it had to do with attraction and desire; it had to do with something very physical, something way beyond my adolescent mind. I had already adapted sex into sexuality before adapting it into a need to be sexy at a very early age because of all the things I consumed through our culture. I had already convinced myself to be as desirable as I could at an early age—because every piece of media thrown my way up to that point taught me that if I couldn't be taken seriously as an individual, at least I could be wanted.

In 2002—when I'm eight—Halle Berry will become the first and only black woman ever to win an Oscar for Best Actress for her role as Leticia Musgrove in Marc Forster's 2001 film *Monster's Ball*—a romantic drama with no romance, where Berry strips down and begs an old, wrinkly, borderline racist, white man to "Make [her] feel good." When Berry had already previously done so much work worthy of this honor, such as *Losing Isaiah,* or in my very personal opinion, *B*A*P*S.*

In her acceptance speech, through tears of joy that may have been pain or an apology that she had to act out this role so convincingly to pave a way for other women who share her reflection to have a brand new opportunity, Berry explains: "This moment is so much bigger than me. This moment is for Dorothy

Dandridge, Lena Horne, Diahann Carroll. This is for the women who stand beside me, Jada Pinkett, Angela Bassett, Vivica Fox. This is for every nameless, faceless, woman of color who now has a chance because this door tonight has now been opened."

There is a glimpse of truth, a great hope, in this statement, but Berry's declaration lacked reality. It couldn't be backed up without a clause in the fine print.

Since this win, this coveted award hasn't been won by a black woman that does not directly relate to her heightened sense of sexuality while simultaneously working so hard at trying to contain it. Although she is immensely talented, Berry's decision to finally strip down for the big screen in a way that was raw and animalistic, in a way that used her body as a container, because who doesn't want to see Halle Berry's titties on the big screen, essentially won her that golden figure—in spite of her phenomenal skill.

There is rarely any form of media that has not exploited the plight of the black woman to make her seem cheap, sexy, motherly, victimized, or used—but always with our bodies as a demonstration as if our artistry does not exist. This is just the reality of the entertainment industry. Mediums such as music, film, video, literature, which influence a large portion of society's ideologies have prided themselves on exaggerating her sexuality and sexual behavior in a minstrel-like way. In fact, these exaggerations have been the force that has allowed women who look like me to be taken semiseriously. In fact, my sexuality has been both the reason for my come up and my downfall—of my praise and my backlash. And it's reiterated through the generations. The reality makes itself accessible to black girls at a very young age when, instead of having simple childhoods where no one should be looking at your body with hopes for the future, everyone around you is constantly commenting on its potential. At your growing breasts. At your thickening thighs. At your big bottom.

Black feminism cannot save me from this fact. Sometimes black feminism feels like it puts me in the position to honor these microaggressive accomplishments my body allows me to receive every once in a while. Whether they help or hurt, no matter how I see interpretations of myself, black feminism makes me feel as if I should be grateful to just be seen, no matter how I'm being shown, because who knows when, or if, I will be considered again.

After Halle Berry thought the floodgates were opening, five years later in 2007, Jennifer Hudson would win an Oscar for Best Supporting Actress in *Dreamgirls* for her role as Effie White, a dynamic singer who's left blackballed and penniless after her music manager and lover impregnates her. In 2010 Mo'Nique would win Best Supporting Actress for her portrayal of Mary in *Precious,* as a mother who verbally, emotionally, physically, and sexually abuses her daughter. In 2012, Octavia Spencer will win in that category for her role as Minny Jackson in *The Help*, playing a woman whose husband beats her and abandons her, leaving her to take care of all of their babies. In 2014, newcomer Lupita Nyong'o would win for playing Patsey, a slave girl ruthlessly and consistently raped by her crazed master, in *12 Years a Slave*. In 2017, Viola Davis would win for her role in *Fences* as Rose, a housewife who parents the child of her husband's mistress.

These powerful women have all played roles—directed by both black and white men—where their sexuality, shining or dimming, stars as the main plot point, no matter how immaculately they deliver these performances. They always win for their pain, they are never happy or revolutionary, they are always punished because they are black, and they are always ruined and gutted because they are women, because society cannot imagine any other way for them to exist. It's like watching a game of who can endure the most before finally proving they're worth respect and care. We can always win as the support system, making everything around us better and getting applauded for it, but who is supporting us, making us better?

In mass media, our women—their bodies, their sassy demeanors, and the way they get what they want—have been presented to the public in order to mold her stereotype into something set in stone. We make ways for ourselves to get ahead and sometimes have to compromise our pride in the process. Not because it is the smart thing to do, but because sometimes we're sexy in a way that triumphs over any ounce of confidence we could ever portray. Because some of our hips are wide and baby proofed, some of our breasts soft and plump, and some of our asses more succulent than most does not mean we have nothing else to bring to the table. Our bodies do not mean we're one-dimensional.

In the media, this is exclusively how we have been forced to proceed. Not because of our overt talents but because of our overt sexual nature. And this may be organic or this may be overcompensation, but at the root of it all, our own bodies have become a force out of our control. We can disguise our control in arenas where it appears we have some semblance of power, but even women as brilliant as Michelle Obama cannot be exempt from being reduced to nothing more than "fat butt."

There is nothing wrong or controversial with expressing sexuality in any way you please. But there is something wrong when this hypersexuality becomes an expectation placed on a specific group of people. We all know this overly sexual prototype isn't true, but our sexuality sometimes stands toe to toe with our success—and even that is policed, for we're still considered jezebels, mammies, or hoes in mediums where we could create the most change—in places where we should be changing the narrative and not succumbing to it.

I think the question that needs to be asked, the dialogue that needs to be constant is: what are we willing to do and not do / why are these the only roles available / how do we say no and still be able to work / who is creating the content / **why are these women all the same color**?

These are questions we have to ask ourselves. In all realms of media, to be seen—to be acknowledged—why must black women be portrayed as oversexed and overworked deviants since the beginning of time?

Saartijie Baartman, a southwestern African immigrant, became the talk of 19th-century Europe when she was transported and literally presented on a soapbox in "freak shows" across England and then in France so that her massive rear end could be seen and ridiculed by the masses—something the likes of Kardashians and friends choose to do today for profit and praise, without embarrassment and without scars.

Yet Baartman's body was displayed for people who couldn't believe the size of her backside. They would arrive in abundance and just stare at her, in awe of the way her glutes protruded. It is said "she had enormous talent" by South African natives and "spoke many languages." But despite her many talents, her sole role was to present savage sexuality without a choice or a say in the manner.

And all I'm saying is it's hard to change a narrative that never had any other storyline.

Black women throughout art and media, as well as us who live everyday lives, have surrendered to ideologies of matriarchs who use sex as a means of control in ways that can be seen in Spike Lee's 2015 adaptation of Aristophanes's *Lysistrata*. In *Chi-raq* women use their sexual prowess in attempts to stop gang and gun violence. Or in a magazines like *King Magazine*, which solely emphasize the anatomy of the black woman, or even in books such as former video vixen Karrine Steffans's 2005 best-seller *Confessions of a Video Vixen*, with which she has built her entire career as an author by telling tales of how her sexuality has opened and closed doors for her inside some of our favorite athletes' and entertainers' bedrooms, documenting the talents that eventually earned her highly popular nickname "Superhead."

These are all overly exaggerated examples, but they are all prevalent nonetheless. I cannot help but think that if any other race of women were so eagerly and easily shown in such a severe and offensive manner on a wildly consistent basis, this cycle would not have lasted as long as ours has. In all honesty, the thought to capitalize off of it probably would've never existed in the first place, but because we are not protected in ways women of other races are, anything goes.

To dissect the harmful nature of *some* hip-hop both hurts me and heals me, because I love hip-hop with my whole heart. I feel the need to defend it because it gets blamed for a lot of bad. But I would be doing my blackness—my womanness—and my sexuality a disservice if I did not dissect its contributions to worldviews.

During the summers, my cousin and I used to stay up at night and wait for *BET: Uncut* to come on. *BET: Uncut* was a popular program that aired music videos with mature ratings. Every weeknight during these summers, at

11 p.m., we would watch videos by artists such as Ludacris, Marques Houston, and Mike Jones. But most importantly, we would watch rapper Nelly's "Tip Drill" video, which song's main chorus was *I say it must be the ass cause it ain't yo' face*. We loved that shit. Why, I don't know.

"Tip Drill's" aesthetic was a plethora of women—black—in bikinis and lingerie or nothing at all performing acrobatic choreography against, and for, every man in the video. The video is basically just a lot of jiggling and shaking and grinding but not normal jiggling, shaking, and grinding. "Tip Drill's" rap video aesthetic was the most advanced version we had ever seen on television at the time. This video is not only infamous for Nelly, who slid a credit card through the ass crack of one of the girls, but it is also infamous for the backlash it received after it aired. Black women had had enough. It became the video that students of Spelman College protested. This controversy eventually caused Nelly to lose out on business opportunities and turned into panels that discussed the detrimental nature of misogyny and the degradation of the black woman, as well as *BET: Uncut's* obsession with portraying the woman as cattle to execute a vision, a fantasy, or fetish for the sake of art. It was one of the first times I saw pushback for something that had become the norm.

"Tip Drill" was my generation's version of every urban legend we heard about Uncle Luke and the 2 Live Crew: a Miami-based rap crew that rose to fame for its lewd language and wild imagery in the late 1980s and early 90s with songs like "We Want Some Pussy." and "Face Down Ass Up."

"Tip Drill" opened my eyes to a world I wasn't yet ready to live in, but it also opened my eyes to a part of me that was willing to participate because it seemed fun, normal even, to be a part of such a spotlighted culture.

Historically, rap has prided itself on being sexist and disrespectful to every woman except they mamas. This rhetoric has been the key element ridiculed since its arrival. The lyrics. The videos. The unprecedented use of bitches and hoes as a greeting, and it doesn't seem like it is going away anytime soon. But because it isn't going away, doesn't mean we shouldn't move some things around. You can still enjoy the music if that's what you choose to do, but we have to continue to call out lyrics such as Kanye West's "I'm in It's" line *Black girl sipping white wine / Put my fist in her like the civil rights sign* or Chief Keef's "You's," *Ain't gone let me fuck and I feel you / But you gone suck my dick 'fore I kill you,* or the entirety of Snoop Dogg's "Ain't No Fun (If the Homies Can't Have None)." We must continue to actively speak out against this casual misogyny, antifemininity, raging homophobia, and entitlement that has corrupted so much of our relationship to not only our men and our art, but all men and all art.

Despite this, what has been interesting is the rise of female MCs who have calculated their careers by taking back their sexual power. Take Lil Kim for example, a powerhouse who became the blueprint of jaw dropping visuals, fashion statements, and lyrics such as "Big Momma Thang" from her 1996 album *Hardcore.* In the first verse, Kim raps, *I used to be scared of the dick / now I throw lips to the shit / handle it like a real bitch.* Kim birthed a nation of independent hypersexuality that had no apparent ties to the classic conditioning most of us grew up under. She birthed Nicki Minaj, who came around a decade or so after and mirrored Kim's unapologetic reflection and reign with videos such as the scorned "Anaconda." A video that received a lot of body-shaming because of its seductive use of thicker women showing off their bodies—the very sentiment that modern-day feminism—or should I say modern-day white feminism—has prided itself on: body positivity.

But when Minaj's body was seen not as a positive image but as an immediately too sexy one, because it benefited her, she came forth to speak out about the lack of intersectionality in feminism when it comes to curvaceous, sexually secure black women empowering themselves and how these same things are given innovator status when a straight-bodied white girl does the same.

Both Kim and Minaj, as well as artists such as Eve, America's new sweetheart Cardi B, and most prominently, Trina—who rose to fame by claiming the title of "Da Baddest Bitch" with lyrics such as *See I fuck him in the living room while his children ain't home / I make him eat it while my period on*—have used their sexuality to their advantage, essentially putting it out there themselves before someone else does it for them without their consent. They have gained control of their sexuality in an environment that shuns it—have gained control in an environment that ironically expects nothing more from them.

I think what's most important is to discover how we choose to let these expectations of our sexuality continue to influence our behaviors and personalities. We have to talk about the ways we water ourselves down, removing all the things that move us, to meet these expectations. We have all done it, and most of the time we have done it for male acceptance. But as I watched a television show and listened to a black man say, *If we gone show off the art, why not the ass too?* as if they were two separate things, I thought, we have to pay closer attention to who's relaying these messages and perpetrating these stereotypes, as well as how much we allow ourselves to contribute in these silent oppressions. A black man, especially, should have a sense of responsibility to us, should have a cloak of security around us, but a man period, should never have the audacity to speak condescendingly about the very thing that birthed him. We have to let it be known that the black woman is not up for auction at any and every turn, not even to our sons, brothers, uncles, or fathers, or any other form of modern-day chain gang, keep masta happy antics. We have to let it be known that our bodies are set at a price that cannot be afforded.

We have to think about what this means to young black girls watching us, watching what we accept, watching what we participate in, listening to our music, watching our movies, reading our books, even if we feel like other people's kids ain't our responsibilities. They are. There's so many little girls who will watch and mimic what I do consciously or subconsciously. I think about what it means to show them that it's important to have a secure sense of their sexuality and body without being ashamed of it, but to also show them it's not cool to be fine with becoming caricatures of it. We have to find a balance, but we also have to find more ways to show the complexities of our magical humanness instead of more ways that show how easy it is to buy us then sell us without equity.

CITIZENS TAKE OUT THE TRASH

When I think of Hurricane Katrina, Spike Lee's *When the Levees Broke* comes to mind with the one sad man of many sad people whose mama died while waiting on a bus that never showed up

How America left her there to expire in real time

Her son instructed to push her body to the back of the line/bus and cover it with a blanket like she was a piece of trash that needed to be taken out

Fifth-grade year we gained these transfer students with accents that sounded like jazz music

With dialects that felt like the bayou and boudin migrating into our Texas schools before and after the flood

And we didn't care what they came through but we knew where they came from and

we begged them to say *baby* whenever they spoke

We still thought it ok to remix Young Jeezy's "Soul Survivor" to fit their reality, to remind them of why they were here instead of home

If you looking for me, I'll be on the block,
no shoes, no socks,
tryna make it to the bus stop

and I could never distinguish if water is worse than a bullet

especially in this motion,

learning to breathe without making noise

learning to live without being seen

with the used to be blue sky that
        is full of blue black faces,
                no stars, we are not in the country where the
                darkness is welcomed, we are in the real world
                where you can't say goodbye when you don't
                know the exact time you are leaving

—we will never forget you are named too many names
we know by heart
Trayvon, Tamir, Sandra, Eric,
LaQuan, Philando, Michael, Dante, Tanisha, Walter, Jordan, Freddie, too many names to name. Christian—Dear Christian, you were 19, you lived up the street from my mama's house, you were too close to home, I didn't know you, but I know you / I feel you holding on to me

Christian you tweeted you didn't wanna die too young, and I know they were lyrics to a song but

Did you meet Emmitt?

Did you meet Jordan later on? He was younger than you

Did they say they tried to warn you but you were already full of lead?

You could die a little or all the way today.

B—you were taking me home going 90 in a 70

    cop cars aren't cop cars anymore, they are big black Suburbans and
Chargers and you ran past the wrong one. The lights started flashing from
both sides—I say, what the fuck is this

When did city cops get disguises?

Both cops surround the car on both sides, both hands on their guns, tell you
to step out of the car,
    you said excuse me,
last night we had just heard about Sandra Bland and you fit the description,
I know you were scared

    black girl going too fast, I know nothing else mattered

You asked why did you have to get out the car for speeding,
me and S asked to hand over our IDs, they do not know you just have a heavy
foot,
    fast means slow to you,
we were questioned about where we were going, we were asked have we been
drinking

They had you out on the side of a Texas road where confederate flags hung
from corner store doors. We took out our phones because we wouldn't let
you die

you wouldn't let you die
They give you a warning like you didn't already have one.

When we get to where we're going, we eat shrimp fried rice and talk about
how fucked up we are and how we don't know how to fix it. *Citizen* said all
living is listening for a throat to open and I am too insecure to say sorry for
what you just went through so we just laugh at everything

I am sorry
    in memory of you
I am sorry
    for what is next to happen to either of us
I am tired
    of taking out the trash just to bring it back in tomorrow

FULL SERVICE

I will never write from this niggerish
point of view again. This is my farewell.
—Hilton Als, *White Girls*

I have on a black hoodie with the words RACIALLY PROFILED printed in white across its center. It's Black Friday, the day after Thanksgiving, and I'm at the airport on my way back to school. I'm selected, randomly, at check in, hands in my hair,

down my back, in my hometown.
Hands never touching my skin, only the
fabric covering it. I'm slightly embarrassed by all the eyes
on me, the culprit. I can hear the *What Did*
She Do's.

This is not a coincidence. I wore this hoodie to the airport on purpose, I always do. I guess they are finally tired of my bullshit.

My hands are swabbed with something that resembles a big band-aid and processed through a machine making a static like noise. The guard, or whatever the person who throws your lotions and toothpaste 'nshit away is called, asks am I ok with this as she takes off her rubber gloves, as she finishes the job. I stare at the machine that holds my fingerprints inside. This is something I expected to happen at one point or another, yet right now I am in shock it is actually happening. She asks again, am I ok with this. She knows, but she doesn't know, I have become accustomed to being looked at as if my face is made of the finest of chocolates—the dark kind, but I am still dirty. She doesn't know that I know she doesn't want to touch me just as much as I don't want her touching me. She never lays an ungloved finger on me. This is something I pick up on and now I am scared of accidentally rubbing my flesh against her tension. I know I will immediately say sorry if I do. I do not want a white girl to feel uncomfortable by my presence. I'm not ready to deal with the drama that will follow if she does. I go out of my way to show my teeth. I have to prove I'm harmless and clean. My cocoa butter lotion will not rub off on you and make your skin look like mine, I promise, believe me. I show my teeth the second time around and tell her I'm fine, tell her it's cool. This feeling is trash. As she throws her rubber gloves away, I don't ask her why she is doing this because I know she cannot tell me the truth.

When I get to Terminal E31, I am met with blue eyes then green eyes then brown eyes just like mine that scurry to the floor in fear I will take a seat next to them. I force myself to conclude it's because I'm talking on the phone too loudly, telling whosever on the other end what just happened. It's either that or the purple braids literally hanging down to my ass. I can feel myself changing, growing blacker in all the stereotypical ways that bring about love and loathing. I can feel myself changing. These braids are so long and separate from who I am. I am tired of being looked at as if my body shouldn't belong to the kind of brain I have. This is making me angry, presenting myself to this terminal only to be rejected. I quiet my speaking voice on the phone, I move my purple hair out of the way, I try to fix my face into a nice one. This anger is blocking my blessings. It never shifts. It is always there, showing niggas what they can and cannot do.

The boarding process begins, they call Zone 2 and I make my way into the line. I am being watched, again, by white toddlers who look as if I am a rare stone they have never seen up close and personal. I am being watched, again, by their mothers who move them out of my way to stop them from engaging with my walk of shame. I am being watched, again, what I do, what I say, how I move in the vicinity of the majority. It is hard for me to pass for I am not a passive girl. They get a pass, for being white, for having manmade authority. They get smiles and welcoming body language. On the other hand, I cannot even publically claim I matter without a *but not more than me* echoing in my autobiography.

I am boarding a plane on black Friday with a black hoodie on and I just got off of my period yesterday. I am feeling empty. There is no more blood left in me to shed. I sit down in my seat and the flight attendant is making jokes about picking your favorite child in case the plane happens to go down. I am sitting on a plane, black—in black pants—in a black hoodie—on black Friday. If this plane goes down, it will land no lower than where I already am on the all lives matter totem pole.

At takeoff, I wrap the strings of my hood around my mouth so I become unheard. There is no way for me to be unseen. As we rise off the runway, I close my eyes and say a silent prayer that if this is my last day on earth, Lord, please forgive me for my thoughts about white folks.

There is, but there isn't, a white prototype; they attack in various ways, they come in different breeds. There are those white folks who assume you don't understand their six syllable words so they give you their definitions midsentence to avoid the feeling of inadequacy they have voluntarily placed upon you. There are those who make it apparent you are their only black friend by telling you stories about how they dated the only black guy in town for a few weeks in high school. There are those who want to see if you have any stories about white folks being racist toward you. They are more interested in these stories than you. There are those who tell you stories of their distant encounters with blackness just to prove they aren't racist. There are those white people who ask how could you say racism is alive when Obama happened. There are those who forget you can still say something racist even if you don't personally identify as a racist. There are those fully grown white men who push themselves up against a wall, cradle their phone against their chest, and turn their back against you when you walk past them on the street. There are those who forget I am just as uncomfortable around them as they are around me.

When I mention inequalities that are within American demographics to my family or the ways of white people or the ways of us, they laugh at me, they think I'm excessive in the way I think, they call me radical and militant as a substitute for other bad words I dare not need to be. They "don't want to get me started," they know how easy it is for me to make their lives a race issue, so they settle for our same ol' conversations. I am bored of our same ol' conversations, about school, about one another. I wanna talk about why all our history was written by white people. I wanna talk about how many lies we have been living for the sake of not causing trouble. I wanna talk about why my black world studies professor is a white Canadian and how she knows more about me than I know about me. I wanna talk about why black people rarely get job promotions. I wanna talk about gentrification. I wanna talk about the issue of white saviors. I wanna talk about respectability politics. I wanna talk about anything other than what we're comfortable talking about, so we talk about nothing instead. And I am sitting in a corner with claw marks on my tongue trying to hold on before I bleed out.

The pilot on the plane just informed us that there is "a lot of weather" between Dallas and Chicago. I like the way that sounds. I'm sitting in the aisle seat of row 3 next to two Indian women, older than I am. We've been in the air for a few minutes, they both glance at me sporadically. I'm sure they are staring at my purple hair sitting in my lap. I say hello and they smile so brightly. We speak and every word spoken between us is about the quietness we feel between our skin tones. The middle seat asks me do I live in Chicago. I go to school there, I reply. Oh, good! What do you study? Creative writing. We are quiet for an entire moment. They both just smile at me as I continue with, are you from Dallas? I know they can't really understand what I am saying; I talk so fast, so long-winded, it confuses most people. I spend a lot of time repeating myself. They nod from left to right unsure of what was said. I nod and smile when they speak, we repeat each other's last words. Chicago. **smile**. Dallas. **smile**. School. **smile**. Writing. **smile**

"So pretty hair," the window seat tells me, and she turns to look out of the window.

I position myself in my seat, sliding down the back of it until I become two feet shorter. I am lost, still thinking about my fingerprints processing through that machine. I wonder if these two women next to me had to go through the same process. I wonder what they were looking for, I wonder what they were expecting to find, I wonder what they would have done to me / to us, if they had found it.

It's 4:21 and we should land at O'Hare by 6:59. When I get there, I will board the loud ass Blue Line on a Friday night for exactly 43 minutes before I'm back at my dorm. I do not want to see my roommates; I finally have black ones this year. Hopefully they are not there when I open our front door, our conversation will only be about the tensions we experienced on our journeys back. I am exhausted entirely by the subject of my skin causing people of my flesh to deal with unnecessary roughness.

While home for Thanksgiving, I noticed my mama had an American flag hanging from a wall in the garage. It was big, white, blue, bloodred covering a big portion of the wall. This threw me for a loop because although my mama has fought for this country, she was never attached to it. She was never patriotic, she never stood up for the pledge of allegiance; she refused to put her hand over her heart. She only joined the military to get out of the monotony of Dallas. This flag was all of a sudden. She told me it was just for decoration. Thanksgiving morning, I snatched it off the wall and threw it under her car. When she noticed it was missing, she asked why did I take it down. I yelled CAUSE AMERICA DON'T LOVE YOU!

Because black mamas can't hold water, when she told the rest of my family who later came over, my cousin asked me where in the world would I rather be besides America because I am as free as I'm gonna get. I guess limited freedom is good enough. What am I complaining for, is what she was saying to me, physical shackles are no longer around my ankles; they are just wrapped around my mind. Yes we have evolved, but we have only evolved into oblivion, into extinction, into the ground. I should have told my cousin this; I should have told her if it were up to whites, to the great grandchildren of these slave owners, black folks would have been gone from this very place we built from the ground up. Is she not seeing how quickly niggas are getting shot out of their socks in broad daylight, does she not see how disposable we are?

> We say don't shoot and they still do it.
> We say hands up.
> We say don't shoot, please, don't shoot me.
> We say it wasn't me.
> We call you sir.
> We say the handcuffs are too tight.
> We say, you ain't gotta be doing all that to detain us.
> We say you are hurting me.
> We say we shoot back around here.
> We say what is the point in asking not to die. Surrender or not, there will still be a black
> poet on somebody's stage eulogizing a dead black body for a white audience who
> pretends to empathize with it.

Before I left home, I told my mama she should read *White Girls*, this amazing book I couldn't tell you an exact summary of. But in it, author Hilton Als says white people expect us to be good at struggling because *isn't that what [we] are best at.* I know she won't like it, I know she will drill her faith into the page, but I am trying to not be best at my struggle anymore. I'm trying to open up new doors for myself. This book is helping me manage it somewhat. I didn't realize white people expected me to thrive in their representations of my blackness. I didn't know how much I had been meeting their expectations. Part of me left the book at home to help my mama get better too, but the problem is that I think she is tired of me making her read black books white people enjoy and feel the need to acknowledge; they are always about the same things. Girlhood. Slavery. Drugs. Sexuality. Our Dialect. Discrimination. The Help. Urban Life. Abuse. Hustling. Prison. Single Parenthood. That is what we are expected to know intimately. These are things white people like to pretend they do not experience. So they praise them, award them, option them for movies, deem them genius. Which isn't to say these books aren't deserving.

For some reason, day in and day out in the life of poor black folks is always more important and credible from our perspectives. It is always believable and innovative when we decide to speak on it, but when we are living it, it is not as important, it is not as worthy of recognition.

Often I am asked do I like white people. I don't know why my opinion on white folks would matter, but I say they tend to get on my nerves way more than anyone else and that is the whole truth. I do not hate white people; I have white friends, ya know, so I can't be a racist. But it is not hard to tell which one's don't like me, and there are more of them than allies. It is easy to feel when you walk into a room, it is a law of attraction, it is the stepchild of the Jim Crow era, feeling like you want to go into a new room with people who look like you. I do not hate white people but I cannot depend on my white friends to do what is right, to correct their friends and family in my lowly defense. My expectations are so low I don't even expect them to. I am learning to hold my own hand, to never let it go, in fear that my fingers will outline the creases of repetition.

The other day my daddy called to ask was I participating in the Chicago protests. A black boy with sixteen bullets inside him deserves everyone's attendance, nothing but distance would keep me from being there. He asked me this nonchalantly; you not out at them protests are you. I act out forgetting whites do not take kindly to blacks checking them. They don't take kindly to black people making sure everything gone be alright despite the fact things are not. But I've never believed in peace in a war zone. There is no peace in my mind. No peace on this plane. No peace in my household. No peace, no pushing.

The plane lands at the time it is supposed to. This is my first time sitting so close to the cockpit, I see whole faces and not features, I see flight attendant's teeth, I see pilots leave the aircraft with their briefcases, I see the inside of the airport through the front window of the plane. My seatbelt is unbuckled, my backpack is on, my fingerprints are still in that machine, if they wanted to they could still find me. I'm ready to go. I walk through O'Hare on a mission to get to the CTA as quickly as possible. I am bobbing and weaving through the crowd, I am walking at the pace of a steady jog. When I get there, I board the next train ready to leave and it is fairly empty. The pilot from my flight is already sitting down when I get on—I take a seat directly across from him—not beside—but across. He stares at me—hard. He gets up. He moves to another seat on the other side of the train—I am the niggerish view.

HOW TO WORKSHOP N-WORDS

In a creative writing workshop setting, the instructor plays the role of choir conductor. He is always seated at the front of the room waiting to direct. Every Wednesday at 8:30 a.m., my fiction workshop professor takes his seat. He always has a stack of papers scattered restlessly around his 1993 all-black Air Max. We—his students—are always seated in a semicircle of rock-hard chairs that hurt my back, that press against my spine four hours at a time. His happiness—his passion, I should say, for the opportunity to teach us how to make shit up in a better, more attentive fashion has yet to rub off on me. It's more irritating than educational. Not because he isn't good at his job but because I can't pay close attention to anything this early. I can still feel the warmth of my pillow against my cheek from the night before. For three years straight I've sat still in these strangely identical rooms, and when I take the time to analyze my surroundings, it is like being in an insane asylum, I must have lost my mind and didn't catch it in time. The walls are stripped bare, so white. Everything around me is so white, but the chairs are light grey.

The process of a story, essay, or poem being read aloud to your classmates to which they pretend to listen and critique for ten to fifteen minutes at a time with words like *flesh out* and *flow* over and over until you forget what your story is about in the first place—is exhausting—is called workshopping. There's a protocol to these environments I cannot disregard nor refuse participation. I'm told this process is an exercise used to discover what's working / what's showing / or what's not coming through clearly in the stories we decide to tell. This is true. It works most times. It makes us better writers, better editors. Teaches us how to pay closer attention to the acrobatics of the written word. Teaches us how to identify themes and undercurrents that could be represented more clearly. So I don't knock it completely.

Today we begin class with one of my least favorite workshopping techniques. Something quite similar to a guessing game, a sort of literary bingo, where our fiction workshop professor reads the first three to five pages of someone's short story. We watch him lean forward into the stack of dispersed papers, pushing a piece of his shoulder-length black hair behind his ear. He picks the pages up one by one, running his thumb through them, squinting at his handwritten notes, shifting his glasses around his nasal cavity. The stories that have an *X* marked at the top of its first page are the stories that interest him most. This *X* represents a personal connection. He's all about intention. He likes a sentence you wrote or a character you created in a way he thinks the majority of us will agree with. He's usually right. He begins to read what the fiction writers at my overly priced private college call "chapter one of my novel." While he's doing this—we—the students, must figure out which one of our classmates wrote it based on dialogue, voice, and other storytelling devices we have a hard time pinpointing at 8:30 in the morning.

This particular chapter he chooses to read on this day is about two teenage boys who have an eventful life as high school drug dealers—a loud pack sold here, a drug bust there. The two characters are having a wild conversation about how "lit" their night was in a school auditorium. For it to be rooted in drama, the comedic timing is impeccable. It isn't corny or underdeveloped like most of the things we hear. It has potential. Style even. I'm not the only one who thinks so. Everyone is laughing at the youthfulness of it all, the urban fiction aesthetic of it all. The genre that is an aka for stories with a lot of black characters, which makes me squirm because I know it could just be called fiction, could just be called literature, like everything else that is well written and involves culture, sex, and violence. But this is not important. Here's what's important: I know it is coming before it even comes. It's just a guttural, immediate, sickening feeling I come across in these classrooms way too frequently. There's no other way to explain it besides intuition. I look around the room as the story continues to be read and try to assume who these pages belong to.

There's a black girl and a black boy in the classroom—one me—one more than my usual set of classmates. He looks like me when I was a little girl hiding behind my darkness. We're the exact same color; he could be the brother I never had. By default, I automatically gravitate to him for mental comfort. I try to pull him to me with silence, give him a subliminal nudge of the shoulder. I'm begging him to say something before it's too late. I'm begging him because I can't do it myself. But all he is allowing me to look at are his eyelashes that stretch out over his face like wings. He's looking down at his feet. He's waiting too.

Our fiction workshop professor is deep into the arc of the story now. He's immersed himself into this world these words are allowing him to live in. His voice inflects during dialogue; his shoulders sway in a different, cooler, hipper way. I think he's about to come out of his chair. He is freestyling the dialect he thinks these black characters sound like and I close my eyes and listen. Wait. I know this boy knows something I don't. I feel him hold his breath at what's coming and I follow suit. Because I know it always comes. We know it always comes. And we know they always, always, go out of their way to say it whenever they can. Because we've never seen any of them prove us wrong. We wait apart, but together.

"We lit . . . *NIGGA!*" . . . Our fiction workshop professor yells out.

He says more words, then "*NIGGA!*" again.

Then again . . . *NIGGA!*

The laughs that were previously in the air turn into thick slices of greasy tension, the swelling is overwhelming. I guess the mere ten of us agree the last thing we want to do is listen to a white man say nigga as if he possessed a second tongue this early in our day. This word affects us all in some odd way, no matter the differences in these ways. This word coming out of his mouth makes us all feel something we would rather not be feeling.

The single window in this room is south of my fiction workshop professor, it's directly opposite his chair. The close-knit confines are supposed to be used as a space to make us feel safe—I just feel suffocated, defenseless, weak. I don't know how to back out of the circle without breaking the trust, without breaking up this minitherapy session by my flatness. Twelve stories up, there's nowhere to go, nothing to see. Outside the window is only a brick wall with brown stains scattered here and there. There are always things around to remind me of who I am.

I feel like they are expecting me to say something, my classmates. Not to defend myself, but to defend them. Like they want me to say I know they're not racist. Like they want to me to say I'm ok so they can enjoy the story again. I feel like these rooms are always expecting me to say something.

Our fiction workshop professor is basking in the spotlight; I can see him glowing the deeper he gets into the story. He is free from his suppression—free from all inhibition. But all I keep hearing is: *NiggaNiggaNiggaNigga*.

NIGGA?

REAL NIGGA.   IS THIS THE TIME TO BE A REAL NIGGA?

Don't you ever forget you just a nigga is all I hear for the remaining three hours of this class. It is on a loop in the center of my skull, it is on fire in the center of my soul.

We sit on opposite sides of the semicircle—the black boy and the black girl. But we are sitting directly across from one another. I can see his whole face. I look at him and think:

I pray this is your story and not theirs

I think:

Can you believe this shit?

I think:

This is two weeks in a row.

I think:

Should ***we*** *be mad because I am, are you?*

This last thought is the one that confuses me constantly.

The black boy who wrote this story doesn't look at me during this entire exchange I'm desperately trying to have with him, but he's in tune with everything I'm saying. We have the same reactions. We speak similar human vernaculars. He really is my brother. He is shifting in his seat, falling out of his black skin. I think he is embarrassed to sit in it for too long. I am shifting in my seat, falling out of my black skin. I am embarrassed I'm not wearing mine well in this moment. *Please be your story* is what I'm saying. It has to be, because then, at least a small microscopic ounce of me will begin to forgive myself for staying quiet. When our fiction workshop professor is done, everyone in the class guesses the story with copious amounts of nigga in it is the black boy's. I don't put a bid in during this auction. I'm thinking. I'm remembering the silence that just erupted in the room when it was said. My anxiety has tripled. I'm wondering, would there have been an internal struggle, an immediate muteness, if there were no black people in the room.

Everyone is right about whose story it is. My professor smiles at our attention to detail. I'm thinking globally, universally, as he hands this boy back his story, why must white people, as an institution, as a well-oiled machine, thrive on taking, on getting ahold of everything, even the name of persecution, even of things they don't really want. I'm thinking realistically, about whether my classmates would have kept laughing if I weren't there. And this thought is the thought that always gets me.

This is not the first or twelfth time I have been in this predicament. I know this won't even be close to the last. The use of this word in the voices of black characters should be expected. This is fine. I am proud of this boy for not straying from its excessiveness, its necessity. This word is his to use whenever he sees fit. The way this word can shift a room when it comes out of his mouth makes me feel worthy of something, of myself mostly. But the way this word can shift a room when it's coming out of anyone else's mouth just ain't right. The way it is casually reiterated from the voices of nonblack readers is high up on my list of suspect, closeted, confederate flag hanging behavior. The eagerness is in their voice box; the affection comes from their enunciation. If I'm being honest, part of me feels like they do this on purpose—he picked this boy's story for this game on purpose. I am past giving the benefit of the doubt. I am past having to teach myself tolerance, past having to make excuses for grown folks.

Maybe he liked the story. The writing was that good. Maybe he asked this boy beforehand and I'm mad at the wrong person. It's a long list of factors I am conflicted about. Did they say it with ill will? Did they say it too confidently? Did it fall too loosely off of their lips? I try to diagnose them before I give up. It's an out-of-body experience. I want to walk out of the room. I want to interrupt the narrative, but I'm not that brave, and I'm not this worthless.

Throughout my years as a college student, I've noticed that beyond what's cultivated by students in class, professors take pride in assigning these texts. The "classic" black writers that taught them something about their whiteness—the Baldwins—the Morrisons—the Hugheses—the Ellisons, in hope of including me in the classroom curriculum to some extent. They depend on them. They read passages from them in class, and then they look my way to complete their thought. I know they choose these black tales to show they didn't forget us, didn't forget me. To show we exist in their lesson plans . . . but if they took the time to ask their singular student of color how they feel, they would know they're disregarding us in the same motion in which they present these peace offerings.

The main problem is the history relived when hearing a nonblack person say nigga. It just doesn't sound good. It is an instantly unstable, volatile feeling that makes me feel unsafe. I think of how deeply respectability politics have played a role in my life. How I've attempted to excuse a lot in fear of something I can't even consciously name. I'm constantly reminded of the ways deep American whiteness always tends to collide with deep American blackness, like we are in constant war, in an unmovable friction, with one another. The word nigga is like a collision that bruises me when my fiction workshop professor says it. It reminds me of how little I've contributed in speaking up for myself and whoever else who needs someone to step up.

This feeling isn't the only factor that changes the trajectory of the classroom. Because it's not like black folks don't know it's said when we're not around. But it's the questioning of do I have the right to feel a way about it. Are these feelings invalid because

1. a black person did write the story
2. it's just a retelling with no intention to harm me, but with intentions that also aren't meant to shield me either

3. I cannot see myself ever giving away the license to make me uncomfortable due to the color of my skin; no matter what word I put on that page

The common excuse when confronted is that by reading it verbatim, they are honoring the author's integrity; they are staying true to its authenticity, as if the only way to be authentic to a black person's work is to gentrify our diction. I'm conflicted by this excuse too. Not in the sense that I don't understand what they mean by it, but in the sense that authenticity is the justification. I don't care how much you are inspired or fond of these black writers and artists—integrity would be to just not fucking say it—authenticity would be to spread the word.

If it were up to me, I would never have to hear any nonblack person say the word under any circumstance in my presence. But when I look back to spaces I've included myself in just less than a few years ago, this hasn't always been the case. I haven't always felt this way strongly enough to say it out loud. I've always found myself in places that were limited to minorities. My schools were majority minority. Spaces where other races saying nigga is just a part of the conversation, a part of our environment. A lot of my childhood friends are/were of some Latinx lineage, and one thing about these friends is they love to say nigga more than niggas. The first time a heard a Mexican girl call a black boy nigga, I was probably in the first grade and I can remember thinking, *is he not gone say something to her?* And it wasn't long after he did what I'm doing now, nothing, that I was being greeted with "What's up my nigga?" or something similar to it. I thought this was normal, my whole life that's what I was accustomed to. I never corrected them. *I thought, they're not white, so it isn't as bad*. But it's just as bad. They do not share what one of my favorite academics Marc Lamont Hill calls, "a collective conditioning known as 'nigga,'" to which he adds, "I'm not saying it should be illegal for ya'll to use it, I'm saying you shouldn't want to use it given everything that's happened after 400 years of exploitation and institutional racism."

I'm on a cruise ship waiting in line for karaoke when a group of white-passing Hispanics get on stage and recite all the niggas in The Notorious B.I.G.'s "Big

Poppa" to a group of old white folks. The rest of the song is not as enthusiastic as the *And if ya don't know, now ya know NIGGA.* When they're done, they get a standing ovation. When it's my turn, I take the mic and make a declaration before I shake my ass to Rihanna. I say, "If you not a nigga, stop saying nigga," to which the crowd stares at me blankly for the entire duration of my stellar karaoke performance.

Later that night in the ship's nightclub, my friend and I are dancing in the middle of the floor when one of the guys in the karaoke group approaches me. He says, "I'm not white, I'm Mexican, it's cool. I grew up with nothing but black people, you know I don't mean it like that. You know how it is." I know how it is, but I also know how it needs to be. I let him know I understand and I know he thinks we share a collective conditioning because we grew up in the same spaces and were exposed to the same things, but in actuality, we don't. We never will. The stakes this word hold for us all will never be synonymous. I had to teach myself there would never be a moment when this word's being spat at him could carry the same weight it does when it's spat at me.

I think about some of my good friends who have used it toward me, how we've used it toward each other. I know there is no malice in their throats. You can always tell when there is. I've been in many spaces where it was. But knowing this doesn't eliminate the fact that it's always utterly uncomfortable. Utterly hard to decipher in its complications. Utterly unnecessary. And this is what comes to mind when my fiction workshop professor says it.

I think, why couldn't he just skip it. Say ninja or something. Say n-word or something. But I don't really want that either. I don't know what I want, but I know replacing it doesn't fix the problem. I just know I don't wanna hear it in any form or fashion—the *-er* or the *-ga*. I don't know how to fix it. I cannot fight entire races of people who use it, but I know the problem still remains because they all think this is an ok thing to do, that it is a new world—slavery is over—racism is over—and times have changed from their points of view so it should be enough for the rest of us too.

Throughout the past few decades, or should I say, as long as I've been alive, there has been talk of black folk reclaiming the word. That's the common reasoning when one who looks like me is asked, "how come you can say it but I can't?" Unfortunately, a simple "cause you can't" doesn't work for the masses. I am not their mama. I cannot control their desires with a lash.

This idea of reclaiming nigga has never really caught my attention because I've been using it practically my entire life. It's probably my favorite word. I'm not gone lie, it most definitely is my favorite word. It has never been something I've had to seek to get back. It just has always been around for me to pick and roll whenever I see fit. But the same hasn't been the case for folks like my granny and other elders I know who have felt the painful beating of the word. And because they have, they aren't in a hurry to get it back, to fit it inside their vocabulary, despite the fact it's never left them. It's not unheard of for some black folks to not use it at all. This is not an issue either. What does cause problems is when there are claims made that everyone, including black folks, should just stop saying it all together. I will never be down with this. I'm not willing to let go of one of the only things that truly belongs to my people and me. It's a very exclusive, very tumultuous kind of privilege. I will never let someone else hold it in their hands.

This feeling my fiction workshop professor gave me is not just something that happens in classrooms, it's in America's DNA. It's clear that there is an obsession with everyone being able to say it because they don't mean it "like that." I think of Quentin Tarantino's obsession with this word his entire film career and Paula Deen's discretion with this word her entire career. I think of the trajectory of rap music and rap concerts where the crowds are mostly young white children and how fixated they are on our language. They live for that shit. But I figure if Eminem can go his entire rap career without saying it, ya'll can hold ya tongue for three hours. I think of Madonna calling her white son a nigga. I wonder if she calls her black son a nigga too. I think of white women with black men who think they've made it past the racial threshold because they have black children. I think of white men who get off on a woman's dark brown skin and kinky hair because it reminds him of the slave and the slave master. I think of how I will never love Michael Fassbender the same way again after seeing *12 Years A Slave* and it kind of hurts me.

It's like America as an entity thinks that if it's able to say it, we have forgiven it for its sins. It's like it's subconsciously telling me, telling us, that if we—us—the majority, can't say it, then what makes you think you can? Maybe the problem still occurs because I sit there and don't say anything about it because I don't know how to go about addressing it except for shutting down completely. Without forcing a muzzle over my anger.

When I leave this class, I've not only workshopped this boy's story, I've workshopped the use of this word three times over in my head. I go to Facebook, a place where hope tends to die. I write a fast-paced status update filled with questions I don't have the answers to. I write: "ok, so what's the protocol on workshopping pieces with the word nigga in it? because i've been in dozens of situations where a piece by a black person is being read by a nonblack person and every time i know a 'nigga' is coming up i'm like just don't say it, say 'ninja' or something and they always say it and then my mood is ruined and idk if i'm tripping or the piece gives them license to do so or if i'm being too sensitive but just **don't say nigga if you ain't a nigga, nigga**."

My friends reply with advice like: *I totally agree . . . it's very uncomfortable to listen to.*

and *girl, you better say something.*

The girl who sits by me in the actual class comments, too. She says:

You know, today in class when I was thinking how in
England no one says that word and how
uncomfortable I am when people read it or what I
would do! I'm so glad for this insight.

She puts a wink-faced emoji at the end of her comment.

She continues in another comment, *see I thought I would refuse to say it, but then I wasn't*

sure if that would be more
disrespectful to your
writing?

In my replies, I keep making it a point to type "LOL" to mask my seriousness. I reply:

see! That's the dilemma I was
having, like is it
being said because they feel that by
not saying it
would take away from my artistic
"credibility?" lol
Or do they just not care that it's a
slur that still
feels like fire when spoken? I don't
know. That's
why I asked the question because
me personally, no.
lol It's not disrespectful at all to my
writing to not
say it. My writing would still be my
writing with the omission.
IT'S SO MANY LAYERS lol.

I don't laugh out loud, or even to myself, while typing this response. I finish, log out, and think out loud, *niggas can't have shit to themselves.*

POLAR BEAR EXPRESS

I met a man in his seventies on the 22 bus. A short, shrinking, black man. African in origin, Nigerian in ethnicity. As soon as I stepped onto the bus platform, I spotted him. For a Wednesday morning, it was fairly empty. He sat in the very first handicapped seat that faced the narrow walkway passengers squeezed through all hours of the day in search of a vacancy. I passed him by with a nod and a good morning, closed-lipped grin because my mama taught me when I walk in any room, I need to speak.

There is something to be discovered about old men and young girls who engage with them in any capacity. Where I come from, these men always wear linen pants that are extremely wide at the ankle and a matching linen button-down. These sets are always color coordinated like a former ladies' man remembering the good ol' days, like a former star athlete who never got over reaching his peak in high school, like a potential sugar daddy. And they always, always, have a cooler in their trunk stocked with a variety of sodas for the kids, cans of Coors Light and a pint of Crown Royal to separate the men from the boys, and some wine coolers for the women. They are always ready to entice. Always ready to tell lies with a straight face and a slight smile to show off their gold-capped tooth. I know the game. So once I made eye contact with this man on the bus, I knew I would soon have to pay for my hospitality.

Nevertheless, I persisted. Walked past him to take a seat by a window toward the middle of the almost empty bus. I'd just left my 9 a.m. class field trip to a sex store where I was informed about everything I could possibly need to know about rubber duckies, anal beads, and vibrator speeds. I was tired. My day already long enough. My stop was the final stop. I was exhausted, and it was barely noon. All I wanted to do was spend the next 56 minutes of my ride not talking, not speaking, not entertaining.

I wasn't even five minutes removed from our slight interaction before I saw him—this man—aimlessly walking around the bus, lost in a sea of hollow space. He'd go toward the driver—then back to where I sat. He'd pass by me—then hover over a couple of seats in front of me. He'd sit, get up again, then peruse my area again. I caught all of this through my peripheral. Side-eying his movement. I didn't want to give him any more leeway than I already had. Yet it didn't take too many more stops before—out of all the empty seats he could have occupied—he was sitting right next to me.

This man sat by me because he was intrigued. Because he thought I was African. A lot of Africans—most prominently African men, think I'm African. I don't mind. They see my skin tone, my facial features, and they assume. I'm used to it. It isn't until I speak, until the countryness, the neck-bone eating, comes out of me that they understand my tongue doesn't sway as beautifully as theirs do. It's never an issue. I'm comforted by the fact we are aligned and they tend to be eased by my southernness. This African man was no different. And in any other instance I wouldn't mind, but my headphones were on for a reason.

His left elbow is touching my right one when he asks, "Do you know where I get off to get on the Red Line?" I don't know where to get off to get on the Red Line, for I got on the bus because I couldn't find the Red Line. But this common ignorance we share doesn't stop me from saying in a tone so convincing, I almost believe myself, "You should've gotten off on the last stop, it's back that way," as I point toward the back of the bus, "You might wanna get off here and walk back." He disregards all the lies that come out of my mouth and continues to converse with my antisocial shell. He doesn't really care where the Red Line is. I had just given him an in. Frustrated, I pause my podcast as he's asking me for my name, and because I'm too afraid to lie to strangers about things I actually know, I say, "Kendra," with another closed-mouth grin—the kind white people give us when we're in their presence making them uncomfortable. The next stop comes; the stop I hope would've brought a screeching halt to this encounter. Not that the man I don't know is a bad man, but the man I don't know is interrupting the plans I had for myself. I'm not thinking about my mama or decency when I tell him he should be getting off now. My nature to be kind has passed. I'm so bothered by human interaction I am willing to send this man into oblivion.

I watch him get up, walk toward the front of the bus and begin to have a conversation with the driver, asking him the exact same thing he asked me. I panic. I know the bus driver actually knows where to get off. I know this man is coming back. I breathe out a breath into the air that suffocates me as I see him walking back my way. When he sits back down, he tells me there is construction up the road where the closest Red Line entrance is so he doesn't have to worry about getting off for a while. Then he smiles at me.

Immediately I feel ashamed of myself, of my quiet assimilation. I thought about what my mama would think if she saw me attempting to treat a old man dirty. How I would feel if I saw someone treating my papa dirty. I straighten my back up a bit. I try to seem warmer, softer, more loving to my fellow brother in the dark wood-colored suit, in the matching fedora, with his wrinkled hands, in some way. Even though deep down I am running into closed closets to be left alone.

He pulls out his brand new Galaxy smartphone. I look down at his hands holding the rectangle. There's an incoming call from an unsaved number on the screen but he doesn't know how to answer it. He says with his South African patois, "Dey keep calling what do dey want?" He watches it ring until it doesn't anymore, something I do all the time. He slightly turns his knees toward mine, tells me something I already know: this phone is new and he doesn't know how to work it. Old people and their lack of understanding for basic technological advances such as touch screens stresses me out. When I see over ten missed alerts on his phone, so badly I want to place a flip phone into his hands and call it a day. Instead I find myself pointing to the red alert symbol next to his call button. I inform him with my finger, "See here, this is all the things you missed. You click here." I click the symbol in the left hand corner of his phone, "And it tells you how many texts and voicemails and stuff you missed. You press it to listen." I show him how to text back and how to make outgoing calls all in a matter of five minutes. Even though I know I'm wasting my time, attempting to show an effort makes me feel better about my shortcomings.

My assistance keeps him going. He puts the phone back into his suit jacket pocket and faces me, asks, "So Ms. Kendra, have you ever been to your homeland?" I think *here we go* and I tell him no but it is at the top of my list of things I want to do if I were ever to stumble upon a large sum of money. I say, "I want to go to Mozambique." We had been talking about it a lot in my South African Resistance and Liberation class lately. Even though it hadn't initially been the main African country I wanted to visit, it was on my mind so this is what came out of my mouth. "What's that?" He seems confused. I tell him it's a country south of Nigeria, a place he tells me he goes home to at least once a year—his homeland. He tells me, "Once you go back home, you will never want to see America again." And I'm sure this is one of the only honest things he tells me during our chat. My response isn't to his statement, but I ask if his stop is coming up. The answer is not yet.

Aware this ride may be longer than anticipated, I ask for his name. I figure, the more I refuse to participate, the more my patience will be stretched out. He smiles at my face when he tells me, "My name is Prince Joseph."

"Joseph?" I ask. And he reiterates, "No, no, Prince . . . Joseph"—his accent thick with pride. I cannot help but laugh at the *Coming to America* of it all. But I ask no further questions and he keeps volunteering answers.

This is what I know: Prince Joseph is a well-accomplished man. A documentary maker, a scholarship graduate of the University of Iowa; he's lived in Chicago for fourteen years; he visits college campuses around the city to recruit film students for his upcoming documentary on African life in an American diaspora. He keeps repeating the word *diaspora* as if he wants me to ask what it means. I tell him my roommate is a promising female filmmaker. He asks for her information, asks me to show him how to store a number. The phone is back in his withered hands. I don't feel comfortable giving out her information, instead I use my own as bait. I say, "You press 'create new contact' then put the number in like this. Press save." I press save then go back into his contacts. Press my number and send myself a text that reads: Prince Joseph. I show him the screen on the phone that shows the connection. I figure he won't know how to find it again. He says thank you, that he will be in touch with her, and continues to tell me about his life.

These are more things I've learned: Apparently, he has a personal chef. A woman younger than him who cooks whatever he wants when he wants. He says he needs her because he can't cook. I tell him he better learn how to take care of himself; he tells me that's what she's there for. Again, I don't believe him. I don't believe anything strangers tell me, but I fancy him. Ask what she cooks and he lists off a variety of African dishes, says no one can cook like his young in-house domestic.

As I sit and wait for Prince Joseph to finish another one of his tales—a woman—midforties maybe. White. Blonde hair. Tired skin. Sits in the window seat in front of mine. She's found one of the last available seats on the bus, which—during our conversation—has been filling up fast. The lunch rush has poured in. People hopping on and off, up and down South Clark Street. When this woman sits down, her ear immediately becomes glued to Prince Joseph's and my voices. I can tell by the way she leans side-to-side depending on who's speaking. I watch her hang on to every word we say. She's waiting on something. A moment. Her moment to interject. Waiting for the perfect moment she can insert herself into my narrative.

Our bus is cruising in the midst of Lincoln Park now—in the midst of white America—white Chicago—where life isn't uncertain, but fruitful. A place where this woman can feel at home in my business. We pass by cafes and habitual coffee drinkers, businessmen in khaki suits power walking to their lunch spots. Its busyness makes me nervous, makes my flesh crawl with its chaos. I get anxious as people are standing shoulder to shoulder on the bus. I look out the window away from the growing crowds. The Lincoln Park Zoo's back passageway is in our view when I ask Prince Joseph has he ever been. He perks up. He's just an old man who has no one to talk to. He replies, "No, have you?" He's been asking me this question every time we pass a big building with big letters on it. I forget to answer. He repeats, "Have you gone there?" "Actually, I have. I went when I first moved here freshman year." I tell Prince Joseph they have a polar bear inside and this is the only zoo I've ever seen one in. I tell him he doesn't have to pay to go, it's a free zoo. He asks, "Polar bear?" And I vaguely explain as best as I can, "You know, like the white bear. The big bear-looking thing but it's white. The Coca-Cola commercial." I respond in references.

He asks me is it worth going to, and before I get the chance to answer, this woman in front of us turns her head halfway to the right, her profile in my direct view, in my way. She addresses the royalty, but really, she's talking to me. "Well yea, that's true, but actually, a polar bear isn't a bear." She does one of those condescending chuckles that tell me she is trying to get on my nerves and wants to me get out of pocket because she knows she has people around to save her. She ends her statement with a watered down version of everything she heard me say for the past few minutes, "The Lincoln Park zoo is really nice. It's free too. Depending on how long you're here, you should definitely go." All of her comments are spoken to Prince Joseph. She heard Prince Joseph's voice and decided he didn't belong here, like he had another place to be. And of course, Prince Joseph, the ever-social man I have grown to know over the past forty minutes is in awe this woman is giving him time out of her day. He smiles so big, "Free, you say?"

I think, *I just told you that, you old ass Negro.*

This only gives her more room. "Yea, it's really nice. Great for kids."

I'm stilling thinking about her bear comment, *bitch, what the fuck are you talking bout.* I don't say anything aloud; I've become more and more prone to causing scenes. I'm trying to be different. I'm trying to stop letting white women get me out of character.

Instead I think about how I've treated Prince Joseph up to this point: with intention to not be as human as I could be. I get angry with this woman for interjecting when I didn't even want to talk to Prince Joseph in the first place. I think of how I meet people like Prince Joseph in these places all the time. They gravitate to my indifference yet always treat me with warmth. I am never mean, but I am always, always, halfway human, with no source of empathy, with clear intentions to not be as present as I should. I'm swallowing the fact that this man who is like a grandpa in disguise has found someone else to just make his day run smoother.

By the time I'm back in the present, this woman is now the one looking out for Prince Joseph's stop. She knows exactly where she's at and where she's going. She tells him how long he has. Engages him in interesting dialogue, all the things I should have been doing. My story about strangers is no longer my own, now I have to share it with her too.

Prince Joseph's stop is up next and he turns back to me for the first time in minutes to ask me where am I getting off. "Harrison and Clark." I tell him, "It's the last one." He turns back to his new bus buddy and asks, "Can I get on the Red Line at Harrison and Clark?" She says she's not sure.

If he'd asked me, I would have said yes, the Red Line is right up the block from my stop. I would not have lied this time.

When it's time for Prince Joseph to get off, he tells me goodbye, grabs my hand, and places his over mine. The gesture is filled with gratitude. I watch him disappear down the staircase toward the El. The woman in front of me is looking at him too. She turns to me, this time where I can see most of her face, and she gives me that gotdamn closed-mouth grin and I go home and take a nap.

BOY IS A WHITE RACIST WORD

black Boy
bullet in yo back black Boy

arm around yo neck black Boy
fist in yo face black Boy
hoodies in yo closet black Boy
durag with no waves black Boy

nameless black Boy
faceless black Boy
brainless black Boy
one chance only black Boy

too many colors on ya body

black Boy
black balled and gay Boy

corporate Boy

boys don't cry but i saw you Boy
around your lips, scared Boy

too scared to look afraid Boy
not bad Boy

not bounty, but bruised
and bruised like every other Nigga

blue black Boy
bullet in yo head black Boy

school2prison pipeline black Boy
fuck tha police! black Boy
always the blame black Boy
ya'll all the same black Boy

fat lipped black Boy
artificial thick skinned black Boy
the last shall be first black Boy
dead black Boy

over ya body, let's pray for the

fathering a little Boy
nigga Boy

unemployed or locked up Boy

crying, noose wrapped
last shall be first black Boy

you black Boy
you black Boy

but you still got a Name
and bruised but mostly Man

DON'T GASLIGHT THE MOONLIGHT

My freshman year of high school I met a girl named Oasis through a mutual friend.

Oasis was /
is,
a lesbian.

This doesn't matter but it's the only way to explain what my problem was.

At the time she had short, bleached, little red corvette hair, and an 80s baby—even though she was born in the 90s—kinda style. We first met during A Lunch. She sat down across from me—to the right of our mutual friend—at the long rectangular lunchroom table we ate at. She had an immediate presence. This confidence that was extremely rare at her age. She wasn't hiding who she was like the rest of us. She also had this urgency to either get to know me or simply be nosy. I don't know. But as I ate, her face was all flapping lips with questions she demanded the answers to. My name. What middle school I attended. What hood I was from. Why did I come to Skyline, our high school. Was the color of my eyes real. (I used to wear these light honey brown contact lenses I convinced everyone were mine, mostly to see clearly, and second, because I thought they made me pretty.) I answered all her questions honestly, except the last one. She blasé'd over my lie and kept digging into my backstory. She kept catching me off guard. She didn't remind me of anyone.

Oasis continued to talk and dig and plow while I vaguely cooperated. I was tired of talking. There's only so much human contact I can tolerate a day and as I was ready to empty my lunch tray, she casually asked, "What chu' think bout gay people?"

I didn't know what I thought about gay people. I didn't really think anything I thought at that age. I knew what my peers thought, what my family thought, and it was all bad. I knew I didn't have any obvious surface issues, but that didn't mean I was void of any internal ones. So what I assumed to be a politically correct response that would separate me from the intolerant, I answered her question with "I don't care, as long as they don't try to talk to me." Not as in speak to me ever, but as in, don't try to make me gay with you.

At fourteen I thought someone could make you gay.

Oasis nodded her head up and down, understanding, empathizing really, as if she had heard this response countlessly and unashamedly come out of the mouths of people so much it no longer fazed her. She continued on with the conversation without bringing up the topic again. She didn't lecture me on fluidity, which she should have. She didn't call me ignorant or homophobic, as she should have, because I was. She just talked to me about other things. Which eventually led to conversations on ambitions—which became our common ground, which eventually led to conversations about music—which became our friendship.

Here's the thing. If I had to make a list of shit black folks are steadfast in not believing in, a couple of things would grapple for the top spot. It'd go:

1a–c. Disturbing the dead / Lollygagging inside of any spiritual realm / Conducting séances

1d. Being gay

Being outraged, unhappy, damaged, oppressed, poor, depressed, abusive, or dead are all commendable existences, but being gay is not. Anything that is not hypermasculine or suspends gender roles qualifies as gay, and the nerve to be gay and black is just disrespectful. I heard the word so much around me growing up that it is both noun and adjective. It's used so much it has multiple meanings. There is no such thing as bisexual or queer or trans or nonconforming, it is all just gay. A son placing a hand on his hip too smoothly is gay. He is corrected immediately. He is punished if he does it again. A daughter choosing to wear her clothes a few sizes too big or her hair a few inches too short is probably gay. A woman who can't find a man to marry her after a certain age must be gay. A voice with no bass in it is gay. A hairstyle can be gay. Two men saying I love you to one another is gay, is causing them to question their manhood, and every man I've ever known believes his manhood is the only thing he has to offer like it isn't an entity in his control, like his manhood is the second coming. They protect it with all their strength, and it is threatened by something as simple as the word no. Which is why they declare anything they deem expository with immediate rebuttals like *pause* and *no homo* after, before, or in the midst of any vulnerable encounter. And the word gay is spewed out

like: poison
like: a death sentence
like: the defining moment

The lunch table with Oasis is the moment I always think back to, now that sexuality and gender are on the front lines of some small scale of liberation. I always think back to that moment at the lunch table when I had no small or grand scope of knowledge and compare it to the space I'm in now where I am listening and learning so that I can confidently position myself as an active ally and not just someone who speaks up when it's convenient. I think about how Oasis shouldn't have ever became my friend at all without an apology. Because a 14-year-old's I don't care as long as they don't try to talk to me sounds at 23 a lot like, I accept you, I just don't agree with your lifestyle. As if my heterosexual lifestyle is defaulted as better, as cleaner, as any more successful. As if my cisgendered heterosexuality is the only thing worthy of representation and open conversation.

A lot of my prior opinions about homosexuality weren't even my opinions. These ideas I had didn't cultivate themselves in my brain on their own. Like most things, they were taught. They were something I conformed into. I had society assisting me. It was my family preaching to me. It was my born into Christianity that was halting me from being a better human. That was halting me from being what the religion's motto claimed to practice. It was folded into what I was reading, listening to, identifying as. Homophobia is embedded into my culture, has threaded itself into our membranes, into our diets. I realized a lot of the preconceived notions I had were rooted in some absurd hateful fear instead of an extension of this freeing godliness everyone had been telling me is so flaw free in its forgiveness and acceptance. All these things assisted in how I was acting and reacting.

I felt myself projecting these policies the older I got. Of man and woman. Of Adam and Eve. Of holy and evil. I had a hard time allowing what I was taught, what I had heard, to actually become a permanent part of me. The things I was projecting didn't feel right coming out of my mouth. I felt like a follower and these things I listened to other people reiterate no longer seemed to fly without disapproval.

It's not unheard of that gayness is the unforgivable sin in the black community. Everyone already knows this. It is what it is but it's not what it should continue to be. It has nothing to stand on besides bigotry. For gayness to be so shunned in my community, a lot of time is spent discussing the validity of it. The who is what, the why are they who they are, the did they choose or were they born this way. You know the bible said the bible said the bible said bullshit. Somewhere along the line my straight ass—problem number one—became the source of reason in my family on the vast topic of sexuality's spectrum when I have no authority over the topic. I'm in no position to be the voice that speaks for every variation of blackness. I don't know shit. It took me until college to learn the differences between sex and gender and even pronouns so I'm definitely no expert. Because not long ago, I was just like everyone else who basked in our straight privilege. The only difference is I learned how to not be hateful. I used to be quiet but now I'm all flapping lips. Now, I am aware enough to challenge the views of people I know simply because I've had plenty of people consciously and subconsciously challenge mine. Who've corrected me when

I've mistaken a queer club for a gay club. Corrected me when I've misgendered someone. Corrected me when I've been casually homophobic by saying things like *he too fine to be gay*. I got so good at being checked that I learned to check myself. So now I don't mind challenging my family and friends. But even within my defense, I know it is hard—borderline impossible—to change people who have used God as a rationalization for their made up minds all their lives.

Two summers ago on a family vacation, my family and I sat around a table similar to the one I met Oasis at. We had a round of spades going on at one end and a game of dominoes at the other. We were eating Blue Bell out the carton, having fun I guess, when inevitably the topic came up once again. I don't know how, but it always does. Out of the twelve of us there, only three of us—the youngest adults of the bunch—defended the people we know and the love they give and the complexities in which they exist in America. And thinking back, I wish it didn't take us having personal relationships to defend before we started to take action in the first place. But in our defense, it didn't take long for voices to be raised and bibles to be found in a house we didn't own and scriptures to be recited from memory that said something about man and woman pushed in my face to be read aloud like I was the leader of a cult. Like I had no reading comprehension skills and needed heavy assistance in the way I lived my life in constant resistance. Everyone reiterated there's nothing written about man and man. That God didn't make Adam and Steve. Or Eve and Eva. I wanted to say that last one didn't rhyme, didn't go over as well. No one reiterated there are gay people in the bible. Everybody acts as if there's no gay people in our family.

No matter how many times or how many ways you explain you don't believe you will go to hell for having sex with the same sex, no one listens. They call it freaky. They call it morally wrong. They seem confused when you mention if that's the case, we're all going to hell for having sex out of wedlock / for lying / for stealing / for coveting / for craving / for wanting anything really. They play dumb when you remind them no sin, if that's what they're blindly choosing to call it, is greater than the other. Which is something I know is written in correct context in the bible—which is, outside the little red words, manmade—but that is another story for another day. I'm not saying being gay is a sin, I'm saying it amazes me how people who are not God can deem queerness on any level as the unforgivable end all / be all, then turn right around and say only God can judge us as if they haven't blasphemously—which is written in as the only unforgivable sin—put themselves in God's shoes without permission.

I made my mama go see the movie *Moonlight*, a movie I can literally never see enough. It's a beautifully shot film about the internal and external conflicts of growing up black, male, and gay while simultaneously being surrounded by folks who believe black males should be anything else besides gay—publicly, first and foremost, and freely—especially. He can be in any mental and literal prisons, selling drugs, mistreating women, getting killed, as long as he ain't gay, he is redeemable. I'd never seen anything like *Moonlight* except for *Pariah*, an independent film about a black teenage girl trying to hide her lesbianism from her very Christian family. Besides that film, I never thought I'd see one about black folks that would be praised and awarded with film's prized possession the way *Moonlight* was. I kept returning to the theater because I kept seeing glimpses of myself and people I love in the characters. Every single one of them looked like someone I know. Which is why I'd take a different friend or family member every time I visited the theater to see it. I wanted to see was I trippin'. Was I the only one affected or did they see themselves too? And were they ashamed, like me. Did they shift the blame, like me.

I took my mama to see this movie because she is the most homophobic person I know. She will deny it because it doesn't sound good, especially aloud so others can know, but it's true. Her black ass is *I didn't vote second term because Obama passed gay marriage laws* homophobic. She is a *disregards gay marriage as a valid and legal union* homophobic. She is an *I'm not Republican yet agree with Republicans on many issues* homophobic. She is an *I'm gonna point out the gayest thing I see in every room I enter* homophobic. I tell her all the time she needs to go talk to someone because I'm tired of talking to her about it. Sometimes I just have to laugh at how much she cares about something that has nothing to do with her. She just stares off blankly as if I'm getting on her nerves. All she knows is gay is wrong and she is right about it. God didn't say be gay, is her favorite answer. I try to get her to not be so cruel. I tell her that her way of thinking is why people are dying. She says ain't nobody killing people for being gay no more, that gay is more acceptable than being black. I show her a list of black gay people who have been killed for being gay. I show her a list of black trans women who have been killed for being trans. She says she didn't know. I ask questions about what she would do if me, her only child, had a girlfriend. Her reply is I better not think I'm bringing her up in her house. This is only a hypothetical scenario. I cannot imagine what a realistic situation would warrant and that is a problem many of us have a hard time facing: the reality of what many LGBTQ+ fight through every single day to stay alive.

I have to remind her she has gay friends. I have to remind her she loves Oasis and Oasis is gay. I have to remind her Oasis has slept over our house in the same bed as me and she had no issue with that.

She tells me that ain't the same thing.

While she watched the movie, I watched her. She surprised me. She didn't flinch or make comments under her breath. She didn't get up and leave like many people in the theater did when the scenes got too curious, got too real, or when gay shit actually began to happen. The bullying, the drug addiction, the strained parental relationship, and the overall trauma of poor people were easy to watch without so much as a shrug, but the gay stuff was where the line was drawn. So I assumed just like those people who walked out, she would start to trip. But she didn't. She cried. But I don't think this means anything specific because she cries all the time.

Moonlight didn't open my eyes to what I knew was already happening in the world, but it definitely opened my eyes to how I was assisting in the pains and bruisings of my counterparts. I began to realize how forgiving we are of black men hurting us, but remorseless toward the ways we hurt black men. This overabundant pressure, this stifled, confined space we hold black men's sexuality in applies even when I'm talking to friends about our futures and what kind of partner we see ourselves with. They say things like: I need a real man. (I have never in my entire life understood what this response even means)

Like: I don't want nobody I have to question
Like: I don't want no crybaby
Like: I just want a strong, manly man

in regards to any black man who shows any sign of weakness, or what they see as a feminine characteristic, as if a man is not real if he is gay. As if a man is not real unless he holds every emotion in his body until it begins to leak out and stain you instead. As if a real man isn't subjective as hell. I know real men who lie. Real men who cheat. I know real men with big balls who are deeply afraid and hurt but their façade of hardness won't allow them to tell anyone. I know real men who need a hell of a lot of professional therapy and not just weed. I know real men who are gay who do these same things, so I am always uneasy about these blind assessments. For me, *Moonlight* portrays in a sense, this outlandish concept of what a real man should be that has swallowed so many of our men in the process of trying to become it.

We like to pretend we've been bombarded and bamboozled with black gay images, media, and life the past few years in a way we have never seen before. We tend to act like it just popped up out of the crevices of hell, but it has never not existed. The gay black community is everywhere. The only difference is—thankfully—the platform has broadened / is broadening to some extent. In recent times, we see the black gay community used as storylines and set in stone personas on shows such as *Empire* and large personalities such as Big Freedia all the time. And although we don't see black lesbian women enough in these spaces, we have black queer women like Lena Waithe creating content specifically with this goal in mind, forming what I hope to be a lane that will remain open.

The main issue is—unfortunately—the platforms can also become pigeonholes. We see gay black men used as flamboyant accessories on reality TV with no hint of relevance apart from their gayness all the time. We see gay black women stereotyped into hard, wannabe masculine figures just as much as we see them stereotyped into the acceptable kind of lesbian that homophobic straight men have no problem lusting after: fat ass, pretty face, nice feet, i.e., someone they find attractive and would like to have sex with. We see gay black women portrayed as vultures who get a kick out of preying on straight women all the time. The main issue is—unfortunately—these platforms do not dismiss inequality. The success and societal achievements of the black queer community are not equivalent to those of their white counterparts. We see the black gay community left out of LGBTQ+ conversations and celebrations all the time. We see Black Pride vs. Pride. We see trans initiatives that have no sense of urgency about protecting the black trans community whatsoever. Even in platform there is still pushback that black folks alike and unalike contribute in large amounts to.

We see the black gay community face oppression apart from their blackness all the time. And through knowing this as fact, us black folk—and I say us, because if you're quiet, you are complying—use these unfortunate events as ammunition for our judgments. We use this idiotic notion of black folks who "add" gayness on top of their blackness as something that can and should be stopped. We see their gayness as a hindrance, as a phase, as a costume that is interfering with black emancipation. As if gay blacks can just wake up and say today is the day they stop being gay and just be black instead because they are tired of living in a body that is a lose/lose situation. We think they can pray the gayness away; we even have the audacity to tell them to pray the gayness away. But who is praying away the right we feel to highlight our disposition.

Some of us are more adamant and volatile in our responses to our exposure. The rappers who are so passionate in their disgust and their descriptions that you can't help but think they possess some underlying desire when they go on these rants of how repulsed they are with having to watch two men kiss on their TV screens every week and how it's negatively influencing their children when all they have to do is cut the fucking TV off if its that big of an issue. Black women are just as bad, reveling in the makeup and hairstyles their "gay husbands" do for them but in the same breath get behind a podium and sentence them to a hell they do not possess. Women who love gay men and "have no problem with them" but will still call a straight cis man gay as an insult.

Although hip-hop contributes to the perpetuation of our phobia, I don't think there's a higher bidder than the black church. The first place I was taught that being gay was wrong was in my uncle's church. The pastoring was completely gendered. Women and girls shouldn't be allowed to wear pants, only skirts and dresses below the knee, always with stockings. We stand up when the pastor walks in like he's our king. We give thanks to the pastor every time we speak. It's a whole lot and frankly very hotep-ish now that I think back on it. These preachers preach this rhetoric of gayness as gravely sinful and straightness as somehow the way we can enter heaven any chance they get, and it embeds itself into kids' brains at an early age. It's hard to unlearn things. Growing up, I've said so many things partially trying to be cool and practically believing what I said because of what the church told me, like: why do you dress like a boy if you don't like boys, in reference to girls who didn't subscribe to the standard idea of beauty and femininity. I've told my younger cousin he couldn't play with my Powerpuff Girl doll because it was for girls. I've many times used the word gay as an insult or a joke or a description. I've let my body be a vessel for ignorance a long while and I don't wanna do it anymore.

In reality, when I've sat in these church pews for hours at a time, what is being preached is the idea of femininity, in general, being our downfall. Not gayness, but the idea of a man "acting" like a woman based on what he chooses to wear, what "role" he plays in his romantic relationships, or how he chooses to speak, or a woman not "acting" like a woman based on those same variables. When Caitlyn Jenner came out, there wasn't a black church in the area that wasn't damning it behind a pulpit because they were scared, the same way they were when Laverne Cox called out their ignorance. This rhetoric against femininity is regarded as the catalyst that dismantled the black family, is regarded as an agenda that is succeeding. These ideas are at the root of these antifemininity rants disguised as sermons, making it easier to use gayness as the scapegoat that broke up our homes.

I don't know one gay black man or woman who has broken up a black family with their gayness. I know mass incarceration very well. I know about the war on drugs. I know about divorce. And I know about slavery even better than all those things combined. But let them tell it, men in heels and dresses is what is continuing to dismantle an entire lineage. I know straight black men break up more black families than anything; I know this white system breaks up black families more than anything. I know black women just wake up malfunctioned; yet we all put on a brave face. We do what we have to do because that's all we ever could do. So I have a hard time understanding what a preacher is talking about when he spends forty minutes on a sermon not telling us what God told him to say, but telling us what he thinks.

When I mention the continuous murders of black trans women, my cousin literally goes from being an alleged ally to deflating completely. His demeanor physically changes as he says, oh nah, I don't care about that. Some black folks can't even fathom anything past gay, and even that is hard to come to terms with. A lot of us don't know. We know gay, but we can't fathom anything else on the spectrum. And a lot of us don't know, because sadly, a lot of us just don't care. A lot of us do not care about making the proper alterations. I had to recently inform my mama that the term faggot is a hurtful, hateful slur, to which she replied, girl, we grew up saying that all the time what you mean. I had another cousin call a woman who came to his register at work *some dyke girl* after she refused to donate to the Salvation Army because of their contempt of the LGBTQ+ community. He replied to her outrage with he's a Christian man and he don't support that community either. He was 17 at the time. Where did he learn this. Who taught it to him. I'm trying to be a person he can never say taught this to him. His mother corrects him before I can. Gets louder than I probably would have. Tells him he won't carry hate in his heart in her house.

When it boils down to the point, you would think the solution isn't that hard: stop being an asshole. I have a hard time understanding how people who know how hard it is to just be black in this world, because they too, are black as hell, wouldn't see queer black people as an extension of what needs to be preserved and protected, instead of being the people to discredit and chastise. Which is why I make it a point to speak up when I can, but every day I am learning to shut the fuck up. I'm willing to be taught. I mess up, but I try again. And I get confused. This is fine. I don't know what a lot of terms mean, but I want to know before I open my mouth to prolong something that needs to end. I'm no longer threatened out of not asking questions, but I also shouldn't expect a handheld tour whenever I'm lost. Humbleness comes with information. I'm still working at freeing myself of semblances of homophobia, which is why we need to let these communities speak for themselves. More important, we need to start listening and processing what is being said. Unity and progress cannot exist when you say you love black boy joy and black girl magic but then exclude a set of our brothers and sisters who are proud and joyful and magical from that narrative. Because at the end of every day, niggas is out here dying. Gunned down. Barrel to the brain and back, no matter the orientation or creed. We have way bigger problems than alienating someone who looks like us based on what they like to do with their privates in private, or in public.

I think often about the hate I've housed and who I've let borrow it. I apologize. If I could go back to meeting Oasis, when she asked me what I thought of gay people, twenty-three-year-old me would just say, Girl, ya'll people too and the world wouldn't move right without you.

THE BEAUTIFUL ONES ALWAYS SMASH THE PICTURE

A couple of years ago I went to Paris—the French one and not the city in my home state. I don't miss being there, but I've been lying and saying I do because people are still asking me about it. When they find out I've gone, they smile at me as if I've been to heaven and they want me to tell them God is real and lives in the crevices of the Sainte-Chapelle. I indulge them. It's easier than having to explain why it wasn't the best experience of my life. I say: I didn't want to leave. A lie. I say: who in their right mind would ever want to leave Paris? Me. After the first week. I say: I had a hard time leaving, that if they go, they won't want to return either. Another lie. I talk about how upset I am to be back. Another lie. I say: it was one of the most picture-book places I've ever seen. This is the truth and this is what they want to hear.

I talk about me, and the language. I talk about me and what I wrote there, and the weather. I talk about me and make things up just to see how much they're willing to believe. I talk about me and books and journaling and the extensive selection of movie choices to stream. I talk about jazz clubs and saloons and the hundreds of wine choices in the grocery store next door to the hotel. About my understanding of euros and Metro trains, about falafel even though I ate chicken, about cheeses, about the wild assortment of breads, about chocolate and how Kit-Kats taste immensely better, about how I don't eat American McDonalds but will only eat McDonalds in Paris because I feel as if their chicken nuggets are made of actual chicken and the Big Mac sauce doesn't even taste like Thousand Island dressing but a wonderful mystery sauce. I talk about the bundles of croissants with apricot jam I ate for breakfast every day, about the Nutella and banana crepes from a stand set up on almost every street corner. I talk about the beautiful faces that could not be avoided. I tell them Paris is more refined, more aura driven, less trying to be sexy. I only say this because this is what I am trying to become. The men are everywhere: bearded and accented, lovely. The women are effortless. I even mention James Baldwin and the restaurants he frequented so they think my writing is coming along when it isn't, but I wish it were. I don't tell them about the ideas I had while there or the underwhelming emotions I experienced. I don't tell them this, because in America I have a responsibility to please without explanation. And I don't tell them how I wish I could trade them out for one another, the illusion and the reality.

Paris for Americans—in a nutshell—is the obligation to participate, the appropriation of Parisian culture, and the overbearing excitement to prove you care about museums. A lot of effort is involved and I don't want to seem unreceptive and ungrateful to my surroundings, but I went to Paris on assignment. This was around the time I had started to take the possibility of writing more seriously. Not just the idea of getting the words out of my head, but how I could arrange them and present them in various ways. I was ready to experiment past my comfort zone of essay writing and instead try different things, make some shit up, get some things wrong. So when I found out my school had an abroad program, I can't say I really cared where it would be. The location didn't really inform my decision to go. I'd go anywhere if that meant I could keep moving toward something. So I can't really say I ever had high hopes of going to Paris. It just seemed like something new—a word-of-mouth kind of aspiration, something I knew no one I knew had gotten the opportunity to experience. It wasn't like the hopes I have of South Africa or the Egyptian Giza pyramids that I've held on to so long. But it was a place far away, farther than the confines of my warm dorm room that would still allow me to pay close attention to the task at hand. So yes, I felt like I was going on assignment. I knew one of the best teachers I ever had would be going as an instructor and I knew I'd learn how to get better. So thanks to the financial help of many of my family and friends, I got to go to Paris for two weeks to take a creative writing class, gain four credits so I could graduate on time, and to write as many things as time would allow; not to be told that the Arc de Triomphe should be important to me when I can't even pronounce it correctly. Not because I could never care about it, but I'm literally not cultured enough to care about things white folks think everyone else should care about just because they do.

What I learned was when in Paris, because you might not ever get the chance to be in Paris again, there is a list of landmarks you, as a tourist, must—and unarguably—agree to visit.

1. You're supposed to go to the Louvre and stand next to the *Mona Lisa*. I deprived my roommate of this experience because I refused to go to another museum and I still feel guilty about it. This was before I knew Beyoncé did it. It probably was a really great experience.
2. You go to Notre Dame and pretend to be impressed by the most famous of hundreds of Parisian cathedrals. I didn't get to go because I accidentally booked my flight a day after everyone else arrived and went as a group. Albeit I didn't care about missing Notre Dame because I didn't even know what it was. I thought it was a school.
3. You visit Shakespeare and Company and buy overpriced books just to say you have the paper sack with the sticker on it, just to say you've been to a place Hemingway has been. (Hemingway and other old white men are supposed to be significant to all writers or they don't really take you seriously.) But even in my less traveled opinion, I won't front and pretend like this place wasn't my favorite group activity. I did love it. Not because of its legacy, but because I'm a fan of bookstores. Although I've seen better, cheaper, bookstores. But in the moment, when you're actually there, it's easy to understand the hype behind it. S&C is compact, with narrow walking spaces and steps that lead to an upstairs where a bed resides. Two of my favorite things, books and beds. It isn't bad at all; it is just . . . a bookstore with a lot of literary ghosts inside it. I regret not purchasing anything, but the broke college student in me kept remembering I could buy any book there on Amazon for one cent.

4. The Metro train. Do not rent a car, do not Uber your life to shit, but immerse yourself into the abyss of fast-paced underground traveling. Also a very great experience. Mostly because a train comes every two minutes, exact. Which automatically caused me to criticize the horrible experiences I've had aboard the Chicago Red Line. Although identical in their purposes, the Metro is way cleaner, way less time sensitive, crowded yet way more respectful of personal space, and way less stress than any other public transportation I've ever been a passenger on. You may see a live performance or two under the train steps in Paris, but you will never see a drunken man taking a shit in the corner.
5. The Main Idea. You sightsee and sit in cafes with coffee and sweets and romanticize this romantic city while thinking there could never be better days than the one you're having right now, not because you feel good, but because you're in Paris!!!

Nineteen other students lived in Hotel Citadines with me, a hotel that resided in the middle of a rapid front street next door to a bodega-like market. Most of these students were also pursuing a passion in the realm of words. We were assigned two to a room, spread throughout all eight floors: eight being the floor I stayed on. I became fast friends with my roommate because she was one of two other black girls there. We had met at the initial information meeting about the trip and she immediately found me and asked to be roommates. We lived together for half a month in a half apartment with half of everything: half a bed, half a kitchen, half a restroom, half a room, until it was over and there was no more walking next door to the Korean restaurant on nights when we wanted spring rolls or talks through the streets while looking for more food about the need to find Idris Elba since we were in Europe, or casting our all black cinema version of Baldwin's *Giovanni's Room.* We slept three inches away from each other in our pull-out couch beds; there was no such thing as falling out of bed without immediately falling into another. In the mornings when I got up, I had to crawl out toward the area where your feet rest. At night before I lay down I'd look out the window and wonder how I got there.

When I got there, a day late and a dollar short, it seemed to be everyone's fantasy around me come true. Just breathing French air became an adrenaline rush for them and all I smelled was cigarette smoke. They all shared something more, something adventurous. I shared the ambition to create with them but not their passion of place. I hate tourism. If I had to sum up my feelings on tourism it would be: unfortunate. I fucking hate it. All the things you have to do and go see when traveling is . . . exhausting. Walking around hours on end pretending to love every thing I see and every piece of food I put into my mouth. Whew, horrible. Do not sign me up for that shit.

Disorientation, for me, seems more authentic. I don't like being guided, I never have. But I did explore. My roommate and I traveled only to find other people who look like us. We hopped on the Metro and went south. The longer we stayed on, the darker the people got. We found Chinatown. We found their version of Little Italy. We found Greektown. We found Little Africa. Little Africa—which was immediately foreign to me, because what we would call Little Africa in the States isn't this friendly, it is just named Martin Luther King Jr. Blvd in the most southern part of every city. But in Paris, although my people are still isolated a world apart, Little Africa is something to aspire to. Living poorer, but seemingly happier. They have small thriving businesses. They are getting by. They speak multiple languages. They adore one another and anyone else they come into contact with. They have big smiles and mouths that are always ready for cheek kisses. They seem better off than we are in America. They seem safer. I don't know what more I could ask for. I started to see why those who chose to escape, escaped here.

Every morning in workshop, most of our discussions were based on recall—what we remember and how we remember it. I remember arriving to Paris, taking my weave out a week in, and I remember leaving Paris; everything in between the beginning and the end is overexaggerated to seem more than what it is: just another day.

Paris for American writers, it seems, equals a paradise—an abundance of material to pull from—an everlasting fountain pouring out words that merge. I get it, why writers who are considered great by the majority tend to run away there. It's gorgeous, every small detail about it, like nothing I've ever and probably will never again witness in my lifetime. While I was there, I wrote excessively and when I wrote, there was instant gratification, an overflow, a pen to paper transference: ink tattooing itself into the flat surface of my left hand. There are two journals I kept during these long two weeks. One of things and one of concepts. The journal of concepts embodies my personality: my ability to create tangible ideas, and how I never follow through on any of them. Just a fish in the water—floating along—alone—doggie paddling in a sea of words I can't turn into action. The journal of things was something I had to do to get a grade, but it quickly became habit. I still write in it from time to time. I welcomed the process, all night writing, writing down thoughts I knew didn't matter, I knew wouldn't add or take away from anything.

- Come back from a gypsy jazz show at midnight, write about how fine the lead violinist was
- Walk in one hundred circles looking for food, write about how tired I am of bread
- Look at the prices for a Moulin Rouge show, write about how "Lady Marmalade" wasn't Grammy award winning for this kind of elitism
- Come in drunk at 2 a.m., write about how I will never drink a Long Island Iced Tea again because being that fucked up is fun for only a little while
- Give double cheek kisses as payment for street vendor, write about how watching *The Parent Trap* remake hundreds of times as a kid really helped me with my European etiquette

Before this trip, I felt the urge to write things down but never enjoyed the practice of it, the hard work required to make it good, the perseverance the art requires. At one point, I made it a point to write one thousand words a day, thought that would make me a real writer, to write every day. My life revolves around routine and routine is something I'm afraid of. I need days off sometimes and because of that laziness, I end up with mediocre work. With work I know could've been better. Always, I am wondering, what would happen if

I took the things I wanted to do just a little more seriously. If I put that extra work in, gave it a little bit more of my time. But I don't because a part of me self-sabotages all day because I'm aware of what harms can happen after the work is successful, what happens when I write something that could potentially change the trajectory of my life, and I don't know if I'm ready for it. I think Paris was making me realize this, which was why I was fighting so hard not to be fazed by it.

I realized that if I fell for this city, like everyone else had, or was fantasizing about, the work I created would be no different than any other thing I've ever read on it, it would just be about what everyone who goes to Paris writes about: the complete and utter awe of it. But my experience, my truth, wasn't starry-eyed. So I wrote other things that seemed authentic to my ambivalence: me in a brand new country with three hundred dollars, living, while trying not to run out of money in a place where I didn't know how to make money. I tried to make this narrative work for me the entire two weeks, attempting to find struggle in everything because I don't know how to be satisfied, even when I was actually enjoying myself.

My first night in Paris our group visited the Eiffel Tower. It even had the nerve to light up for me, all golden and glistening under the moonlight. I was annoyed by its lack of normalcy, at how easily it stood out. We took the elevator inside and I stood in the middle deck looking down on the world. I felt an obligation to make sure everyone back home knew what I was doing, to make endless declarations on social media about how happy I was to be there. I felt an obligation to listen to "Niggas in Paris" at least once—the only concrete goal I made for this trip. I had to take pictures at Montmartre, in front of the Moulin Rouge, pick any building and it will give you the effect you want. I did all of this to remember to not forget being twenty stories above this city. I brought everyone I knew a souvenir back just to say I made it, because they know, just like I know, *we ain't even supposed to be here. We*, me. Black. Broke. The first of people I know who have ever been this far. On the wrong side of privilege.

I was in the grip of dreams that almost came true
I was on the cusp of finding out what it meant to be inspired
I was on the cusp of making this habit, making it second nature
    A form of self-diagnosis
    (We have to stop naming things) Just because things are new does not mean they are life changing

On my flight home, I started my period. It seems that every time I'm supposed to get on a plane, my uterus begins to overflow and I still pretend to be surprised by it. For ten plus hours I sat in a window seat—with no pads, no change of panties, no ibuprofen, no immediacy—next to a man who got tired of me waking him up out of his turbulence dependent sleep so I could get to the lavatory despite my spite about public restrooms. I sat there with just a stack of tissues I traded in for paper towels every couple hours stuffed inside my leaking body. Falling asleep, on and off, unaware I could've asked the stewardess for assistance, listening to the bottom row of my teeth grinding against the top row. My jaw gliding to a steady rhythm breaking down the pain, making the discomfort become more self-inflicted rather than incidental. My customs card I never filled out due to its complicated survey of questions is still in my brown journal: the fancy one that looks like its skin is from a dirty alligator. The fancy one that is still half empty. I didn't know who I was, or what I brought to the table besides a bottle of wine to properly fill out the sheet.

As I stood in a line that seemed to be moving way too fast, they told me if I was American, I didn't have to fill it out to enter back into American civilization, just to have my identification ready.

"Where are you coming from?" the customs man asked me as I handed him my passport.

"Paris."

"Cool." He said, as he handed it back to me without even opening it. He didn't even care about where I had been and it made me feel good.

DEAR LIFE

Movies without sound
Legs, intertwining

I will not give in to you
You will not give up on me

SKIN CRACKS, BLOOD SPILLS

I'm standing in the medicine aisle at Target. I'm always in an aisle at Target. Every couple of months, the Chicago air makes me sick, and still, I haven't trained my memory to learn what it is I need for a common cold. Pills, cough drops, an inhaler, some codeine, more than likely just a good nap. A good nap solves congestion. A good nap can solve anything. Which is why I'm in the aisle staring at what's in front of me, trying to find something that will help induce this good nap. It's so much stuff. I bring my hand up to my face, my forehead, and scratch. I cough. Then sneeze. The variety, the possibility, of making the wrong decision makes me nervous. This may just be homesickness. I cover my mouth with my free hand and cough into it. I listen to the skin on my face crack as I scrape up and back and forth. The skin I peel off cakes under my fingernails. I've consumed the outer layer of me even with a gallon of water a day in my body; I know I will never have clear skin. This is what they told me it'll take. Water. But my face still has the consistency of a chocolate bar with nuts. I will never glow in the dark. My face keeps caving in like an uneven road that squeaks under the weight of tires. I rub the blood back into my pores and keep scratching, keep tugging until I see craters.

When my phone rings, it's my mama. When I answer, she doesn't say hi, she says, Girl I just got off the phone with A. A is my aunt. I sniffle. My nose is clogged. I know there is a story following. I prompt its start,

What she want?

Girl—she begins—calling, crying, talking bout she bout to kill herself.

Kill herself?

Yea, she confirms.

You going over there?

Naw I ain't going over there, I'm at work. She ain't bout to do nothing.

How you know what she gone do, I say as I grab Theraflu off the shelf, it's berry flavored. I read what the medicine is for: severe cold and cough. Headache. Sore throat pain. Runny nose. Body ache. Cough. Fever. Alcohol Content: 10%. That's more than some wines. I plan on drinking the entire bottle. I fit the description. Clogging has been stopping up my chest since I was a smaller girl.

She just ain't got no money to smoke, girl she do this all the time.
I stop replying but she continues,
A ain't fooling nobody.

I tell my mama I'll call her back. My hand is back on my face. My fingertips are scurrying around my eyes, up my nose, around my mouth, trying to find a spot raw enough to unwrap. I set the Theraflu back on the shelf. It's tea, not syrup. I don't drink that shit unless it's sweet and from Texas. I go down the aisle a little farther, stand in front of the cough drops and try to find the cheapest, most effective brand to try and get my mind off one of my favorite women possibly being dead. I think about her dying all the time. I think of everyone dying all the time. What songs she would want played at her funeral. I always think of her corpse laid out to 90s R&B, maybe Jodeci's "Cry for You." Or maybe she'd want Robin Thicke's "Lost Without U" to play. I don't know. She loved a variety of things, but every single one of them were predictable.

This is what I'll tell everyone at her funeral, in my eulogy: I always thought the crack would be the one to take her out. That she would choke on her own high. That her addiction would run its course. I'll tell them I never thought about her being her own killer.

While completing a research project on drugs in inner cities, I read a news headline that said, *Is Crack Back in 2015?* As if it ever left the front porches of black homes. I'd be hard pressed to find a black family with no crack addicts in it. They asked if crack was back as if the 1980s, the CIA, and Ronald Reagan never happened. They asked if crack was back as if the aftermath of flooding the inner cities of California streets with crack cocaine was just a chapter in America's history instead of a first step to destruction.

I wasn't born during these times to witness crack at its height, but a couple of decades later I saw the breakdown of the substance from various points of view: the dealer, the addict, the distributor, and even from a literal standpoint, in 50 Cent's 2005 film *Get Rich or Die Tryin'*. I saw the characters in the movie concoct the drug with their bare hands. I saw them reduce cocaine powder by cooking it with baking soda and water and turning it into an 80% purer drug, turning it into a solid rock, and when people smoked it, they got higher for half the price and called it freebasing. I saw them distribute it and disrupt the lives of many. I saw them profiting off its sale. As an 11 year old, I thought the science behind it was cool, the hustle behind it was understandable. But through being a nosy child and asking questions about my aunt, I knew I was missing something that didn't seem right. I heard people saying selling drugs was wrong, but something in my mind wasn't comprehending the depth of why they continually said these things. It took me reading and asking even more questions to learn that this drug was introduced to these communities so the masses of unemployed black men and their poor black families could fizzle out while simultaneously providing a means to make money. And because of the predicament of those citizens, our government knew their bait could be disguised as opportunity. The introduction of crack to black America was used as a gateway to find new markets to sell cocaine's poor sister in, and this poor sister just happened to be one of my aunts—my mama's sister. So maybe the headline should've read instead, *Whitney Said Crack Is Waak, Not Crack Is Back*.

To test out the drug's gravitational pull and strengthen its fan base, free samples of crack were given to occupants of housing projects and other poor neighborhoods. In 1985, my aunt had her first hit of premo: weed laced with crack. She lived in Oak Cliff at the time, an inner city neighborhood in Dallas generations of my family have occupied. This same year, her sister's things would miraculously disappear out of my granny's house: shoes, TVs, jewelry, money, meat out of the freezer. By the time crack's marketing had been perfected, members of these families were already drug dealers and/or users of the substance. And soon enough, the highly potent substance was everywhere. Selling as cheaply as five dollars a hit.

In late 2016, my aunt still owed her dealer. She gives her daughter her government checks every month to hold so she won't spend her rent money on small rocks.

As I stand in the medicine aisle, unable to focus, rubbing the back of my hand across my wet nose, I scroll through my contacts and dial: GRANNY. My aunt has my granny's cell phone; she let her keep it so the family can stay in touch with her. She answers the phone quickly. It barely rings, as if she was waiting for me. I say hello. She says, Hey niece. I ask, What's wrong with you? It is the furthest it can be from a question. She's already crying. It's not the realistic kind of cry where I think tears are falling. It's more of a hopeless desperation. A pain of coming down. A pain of unwelcomed withdrawal due to lack of funds. If this continues on until the next day, she will become mean, inconsolable, only out to puncture whoever is in the way of her next hit. When she's like this, she becomes childlike, confused, dependent. When she's like this, it is hard to be around. Because crack's euphoria only lasts a couple of hours, to stay high, she has to smoke numerous times a day. Her surroundings contribute to her access. She lives in a drug-infested apartment complex that she's soon to be put out of. Back in the day, during the height of crack, these crack-infested communities were so dependent—both financially and physiologically—on the drug, the confinement and enablement of those home atmospheres did not matter. It still doesn't matter because once addiction forms, time doesn't matter.

Crack got its nickname because when smoked through a pipe in its rock-shaped solid form, it makes a crackling sound. My aunt smoked out of a pipe for the first time in 1988. By the end of that year, her second child was born.

In 1989, a study found that 1 in 6 babies born in Philadelphia tested positive for crack cocaine, therefore birthing the term crack baby, a baby who is not strong or healthy enough at birth due to the mother using crack during pregnancy. My aunt has been addicted to crack longer than I've been alive. Longer than one of her children has been alive. I've never met her as anyone except who she's been. She has always been the funniest person I know, who loves me like I love her, who leaves me voicemails about shit she knows I'll laugh at, who calls me to check on how my dog is doing.

When I'm on the phone with her, my voice cracks. Not because I'm sick, but because I'm kind of sad at the possibility of what could happen to her at any moment. I ask her why she wants to kill herself. I want to ask her why she keeps killing herself. She says she wants to smoke but she ain't got no money. I ask why she just won't stop and she says, I can't! She says her sisters don't believe her, that she'll do it. This is her threat. I tell her I know. I tell her to come over my house. I'm away at school, but I still invite her into my house, my mama's home. Her voice cracks this time, she says ok and she sounds like a scared child. She says she will call me back. She says she wanna die because she's tired of smoking. I cough in her ear. I'm thinking about the times we visited her in jail. The only time I've seen that many black people in one place is either at church or a barbeque. I tell her ok. I'm thinking about all those times we visited her second child in jail around the same time we visited her. So many men unaware of the possibilities.

In 2015 black men on drug charges occupied over 60% of state prison spaces. Black women historically outnumber black men, and black people as a whole only occupy about 14% of this entire country. Something about these numbers is staggering, never making absolute sense, but in the context of how drug laws are created, makes complete sense.

In 1986, a crack house law was conveniently passed, making it a felony to open, lease, rent, use, or maintain any place with the intention of distributing any controlled substance. A trap house law. A black ass law. A war on the drugs black folks like to consume. If caught distributing, the dealer could face up to twenty years of prison time and/or fines up to $500,000—a law where consequences were not the same for black and white sellers and users. For white drug users with money, their drug use is rarely punishable by law. In fact, there is a 100-to-1 disparity between white power distributors and black crack cocaine distributors. Powder cocaine is the high-end drug, the white drug—literally and figuratively. Snort cocaine and you go to rehab, smoke crack and you get life. This law was passed two years after crack was introduced, in retrospect, with the hopes to encourage distribution. The same people who began selling drugs to make a living would now be expected to pay a $500,000 fine and/or go to prison for the very thing they were encouraged to do.

Statistically, 1 in 9 black children have a parent existing behind prison walls on a nonviolent charge, compared to 1 in 28 Latino children and 1 in 57 white children, which leaves a lot of half-full homes in need of emotional and financial support.

Imagine waking up one morning to an empty house, which is what a lot of children with drug-addicted parents have done, people I know have done. These children spend a great portion of their lives raising themselves. The fathers gone for selling drugs. The mothers gone for using them. Parents that disappeared into alleyways and prison cells way before they were able to comprehend what has happened to their family. It took me up until now to understand what has happened to mine, a reiteration of black disposal.

When I call my mama back, I still haven't figured out what medicine will make me better. Something like livelihood has infected me. Poison keeps getting thrown in my body. It's like a cavity, too sweet, but too bitter to swallow. I put a pack of Target brand cough drops into my cart and decide to take a surplus of Tylenol 3s when I get home. When I tell her what her sister said, my mama's voice is even, unbothered even. She repeats her previous sentiment.

Girl A ain't about to do nothing.

I make her agree to let her stay over the weekend, to pick her up when she gets off work. I bite my nails down to the cuticles. The cuts burn when they hit the open air. I tell her she sounded forreal. My mama tells me I don't know her like she knows her. I hang up.

I call my aunt back before she has the chance to get back to me. I tell her my mama said she can come stay for the weekend. I'm trying to show her we care, that we care if she lives. But she has overcome her hysterics. I catch the caution in her throat as I present her with a way out. I can tell she's over her uncertainty. First she tells me her daughter, my cousin, is on the way to pick her up. Then the story changes. She tells me she's just gonna stay home. I hear a ceremony in the background. A chain of voices going up to the ceiling of her small apartment. It's a deep voice speaking, I can feel it in the center of my stomach. She says C came back. She says she'll be ok. I can hear her teeth chattering, her jaw sliding back and forth. She's high.

I pick at the flaky skin on my chin in the aisle I'm still standing in. Not moving. Not growing. Not getting stronger. I create a crevice where my blood can fall out easier. I roll my eyes and rub my nose; I tell her sickness don't have to last always. I tell her life is about choices.

MAMA SAID ON MOTHERHOOD

you hold your stomach—that little girl crying at your feet
that little girl biting your hand off of your broken body

you blow her away, let her fall to her knees, tell her she isn't worthy of your
love
you let her scratch at your ankles as you pick up your pride

and

joy as you weigh your choices in front of their faces
they watch you in unison, they watch you—

you like them as much as you like yourself
they see your third eye blackened by your blurred vision by fists by
prisons

they see mama holding them at an angle wider than arms stretched out
to thee

they see themselves in new beds tonight with dirty sheets
they see police stations and cps agents
they see daddy, refusing to love mama refusing to love them
they see stop! and no! and be quiet! and what's wrong with you! and
cracked cement and water splashing in your ears

and contrasts of unrequited wombs and baby got the blues at two a.m.,
they yell into tile floors—they

pacify themselves then pull the plug

at two a.m.
she knows when to say sorry

at eight a.m.
she knows how to say love you

at 2:40 p.m. bags are packed at the door

transporters—time consumers—lying on the floor—his hand back around your throat—shape shifting. you can't come home without a thank you note. you wonder if you love him more than you love them

THE CHEAPEST CASKET

When my mama dies she wants to be buried wrapped warmly inside a single white sheet—like an afterbirth. She wants the sheet to start around her head, covering her halo of brown, thick hair then continually wrapped in a clockwise motion around her body, down to her toes, until she becomes a cocoon and nothing but the front of her face is visible—like Jesus in the manger. I have pictured this image and other images of her being gone untimely and harshly, way out of my control—me at her funeral making sure no one laughs at my baby Jesus. I believe it will be sudden. All of it. Her death her funeral how soon I will forget her. I would rather it be sudden. I do not want to watch her go over a period of time due to a sickness or a disease. Due to cancer or Alzheimer's. Due to her kindness. I don't want to have to beg her to stay, because I will. **I will plant bombs in the tombs of my soul and there will be no remains left if she leaves me here alone. She is my home.**

About four years ago we exchanged funeral preparations on a piece of notebook paper. This was after I got sick but didn't die, and in an attempt to make me overlook the safety net that almost forgot to protect me, she suggested we plan out our death celebrations instead. I have since misplaced her copy of demands but I've memorized exactly what she wants, it isn't very complicated, just unconventional and maybe entertaining if I'm able to get in touch with Shirley Caesar.

My mama's not afraid to die. At first I was, I used to be, some days I still am. I'm not ready to die. But I am reminded death doesn't matter, it's just uncontrollable: being separated from the body does not mean you are dead, or dying.

Being separated from your body just means you are moving on from a place that can no longer hold space for everything you were to fulfill.

Two weeks after my first semester of college started, I got sick. For a week I could not move out of my bed without feeling as if every intestine in my gut was being clipped piece by piece by scissors that just couldn't get all the way through the first time, so it pricked and pricked until finally separating them into finger puppets. I would just lie there in stillness for days. No appetite for food and only a couple sips of water each day. There would be no movement for minutes at a time then sporadically, the clipping and stabbing would occur until I was bent over backward, biting my pillow so I wouldn't curse and say God in the same sentence. After the third day of endurance and overcoming my fear of making my own appointments, I finally went to a doctor who could not explain my symptoms. He was only sorry I was in so much pain. He didn't know what else to tell me, to do with me. They took blood and as the needle went into my veins, my body went cold. Ice started to rise from my toes and still me in the moment. Heat began to fire out of my ears, back down through my ribcage—these opposite sensations met in the middle of my torso before the collision caused sweat to fall down my face and my eyes to close shut. They could not explain this either. They sent me home. When I left the doctor's office, I walked around downtown lost. Still nothing but a new girl to the city, looking for my dorm. I thought I was going to die on one of those backstreets.

At 1 a.m. that night, when I was back in my normal position, legs and arms spread out as far as my body could stretch to subdue the pandemonium that was inside my stomach, my doctor sent me an email with the results of my blood test. The email said my blood was on the verge of clotting, around the lungs. The levels were fatal, he said. *Fatal.* I was advised to go to an emergency room right away. I went the next morning.

Right away I had to call my mama and tell her that her only child was about to die. I didn't know how to do it without sounding scared. I was taught not to be scared. I didn't want to sound scared: mama they said that I'm fatal **I try not to kill her before she dies** and I have to go now. She said she would be there by morning. She was telling me not to worry, everyone was gonna die.

In the emergency room, five doctors stood around my bedside, staring at, and touching my abdomen while my mama sat in the chair next to me, staring at them.

"Does it hurt when I touch here?" one of them asked.

From the opposite side, another man asked, "What about here?"

"No." The pain is on the inside it is pain it is painful I can't breathe.

"We will go run some more test, we do not think it's cancer" said another.

I did not think it was cancer it is not cancer it is a step up from childbirth I can't sit straight I haven't ate in four moons I'm beginning to see my spine, sir.

"We will get you out of here soon."

Someone in my family is going to die soon. If it is me I am ok with it. Soft crying. No pleading. Only accepting I was made to only exist for eighteen years. I began to think about babies and the ones that were soon to be birthed into my family. My cousin was nine months pregnant. It is said when babies are born, someone dies. A life for a life. But then it is said—meaning what I've been told—people tend to die in threes. Maybe it is months apart or weeks or years, but three. Three deaths and we strike out for good. My family is not big enough for one person to stand alone.

My mama and I are always trying to figure out who: a distant cousin, someone closer. Through process of elimination we try to figure out who it might be by who has done the most dirt, who has lived the longest life, but most times we conclude we'd rather it be one of us instead of one of them. We race between one another. If I go and she stays, fine. If she goes and I stay, I do not know what will happen to me.

"If it is me . . . ," she always says.

"As long as it's not my mama." I always say.

They come back—the doctors—together, to touch me some more. They pretend to look at my chart with concern. The white walls have become paler since the last time they were in the room. My mama watches me watch them.

"We couldn't find anything wrong with you. If it doesn't pass, come back and see us."

Make something up then. It hurts I know that you can see something is not right but there is nothing wrong with me. They say I will not die I will just live through this blood dripping from my heart when you leave me here, mama.

There was a story I was reading about a mother who thinks either/or, much like my mama. No explanation, just cut and dry. If she believes something then the contrary of her belief must be bad and you must not believe it because believing in the wrong things and in the wrong people is how you book a one-way to hell. But really, she is my only friend. I depend on our closeness. There is nothing or no one who knows that our problem is we spend too much time. And time only makes room for truth. No matter how strong my mama thinks she is, or how strong I know she can be, she cannot handle some truths, the bare ones, the ones that make her question what she is willing to stand for. When we leave the emergency room, she takes me to get some food, she makes me eat pasta I do not taste. It tastes like I'm eating empty space. Like I'm chewing on my tongue so I won't say anything mean. We talk about what the doctors said, which was nothing. We talk about family back home and when she planned to go back. I make a comment that "they" get over on her—as in people we both know. I said it because I meant it. She shifts all the way in her seat. She waves my comment off with her left hand, "I'm done talking to you."

"What."

"How they get over on me."

"Well, getting over is the wrong word. My bad. They take advantage."

She silently picks at her food. There are certain people I can't openly talk about with her. We can talk about her dying or me dying but we cannot talk about the lives we are living.

"Yea" she says, "Everybody takes advantage. Everybody."

"Oh, so you including me in everybody. That's what you doing." Almost a question coming from me, hardly.

"Yea, ain't that what everybody mean."

When I was sixteen this woman approached us in a restaurant while me and my mama were having a disagreement. She didn't say hi, she just said she overheard us. She told me the day her mother died was the worst day of her life. Just her mentioning it caused her to tear up, caused her to feel it again. Or maybe she'd never stopped feeling it. She told me to be grateful. My mama told her thank you.

I leave the rest of my pasta in the plate and pay for our meals. We go home.

I do not tell her I would die for her without anyone asking me to. I do not say anything on our bus ride back as I lay my head in her lap to cry from the pain she just added to my insides.

When we exchanged funeral preparations it was fun. We sat in my room and I looked up at her from the floor as she sat on my bed the night before her flight home. It was fun because of the major differences we had in the expectations of the people we will leave behind. Mostly of one another. I still have to think about if I would actually wrap her in a sheet when she goes. It seems to be a constant whenever we talk about it. She wants to wear a sheet. I want to wear what I would wear to sleep, a t-shirt and baggy bottoms since I would basically be taking a forever nap. She wants a eulogy preached by a pastor who shares her same values. I want everyone there to say something about me, preferably something true. She wants "Heaven," and I want "Jesus Walks." We begin to trade ideas. "Do not spend a lot of money on no casket. Buy the cheapest one they got and bury me in the veteran cemetery. It's free." She always says there is no need to spend that much money on dead people. The body isn't something that needs to be preserved.

"So a wooden box."

"I guess. Whichever one is cheapest," she reiterated, "and don't let certain people come."

For a long time I did not know I wasn't supposed to fear death. In movies, that is the number one thing the characters try to avoid. They jump over buildings, slide under cars, anything to avoid the hit. Death, in the bible, romanticizes its essence in a way it seems almost revolutionary. In life, death is the one thing we cannot run away from. My old pastor said life after death is better than life on earth and I don't know how he knows when he hasn't died yet.

I have concerns. Will I know the same people in heaven as I do on earth. Will I even go to heaven. Will my heavenly family be the same as my earthly one. I have faith **Mama, I don't think I'm good enough to be able to meet you in heaven. I have too many secrets I have kept from you.**

"Do you love the Lord?" she always asks me.

"Yes."

"Well you'll be in heaven."

The scary part of dying, for me, is the how. The how is more important than the when. How will I die. When I was eight, I thought the best way to die was in your sleep. I was sure it was the way I wanted to go. Easy. Smooth. Uneventful. Just die all on my own. Now I know the simplicity I'd hoped for wasn't as profound as I had made it seem. Things go in mysterious ways.

Nobody talks about their own deaths but it is so close I see nothing besides it. Death is my favorite subject and subconsciously, talking about things aloud, the results either tend to drift away or come to pass. I hope I am not speaking anything into existence about my existence. I do not want to drown / get buried alive / murdered / I do not want to be a victim. I heard brain aneurisms are quick, but painful. Pain doesn't scare me though, not being in control does.

When my great grandmother died she was over the age of ninety. She was not wrapped in any white sheets, she didn't even have an open casket, but it was expensive. And she was probably scared. She didn't remember our names anymore but she was scared. I do not want to be scared when it is time for me to die. I think I saw my mama cry a small amount of tears at her funeral, then she got up and said her goodbyes. She said she'd do the same when I go but I don't believe her. Then she said most likely she will go first anyways so there would be no need.

When my mama dies, I am instructed to do everything I would do if she weren't missing, which seems impossible. It has been almost ten years since someone in my immediate family has passed. She thinks she is next. And every day it feels as if we are closest to a visit. It is unthinkable, the thought.

When my mama dies, I will fulfill her wishes. I will wrap her in more than one white sheet so that I know her spirit is safe. I will remember those times I would come home on breaks, most nights sleeping in her bed. I will remember when she got up to go to work in the morning how she would tuck me back in because I am / I was, her husband.

If you die while I'm here, mama, while I'm in a land of buildings that hold each other up, please do not let me down, let me go first.

If I am still living inside the body while she's outside of hers, help me.

BOMBS ON FIRE

My daddy and I always end up watching movies about war. Movies where people are blown to pieces. Movies about people living in pieces. Movies about white men playing God while simultaneously losing their everlasting mind trying to stay alive and functioning. Movies such as *13 Hours: The Secret Soldiers of Benghazi, Stop-Loss, Forrest Gump*, or fan favorite, *Dead Presidents*—albeit not many white faces, but still balancing itself on this same survivor's instinct. We watch them on purpose. Predicting the plot's future is what we call a good time together. The anticipation we share for violence, for anger, and the inevitable unraveling of the protagonist's psyche intrigues us—despite knowing these films could potentially give my daddy flashbacks. Seeing as how every time we watch one, he spends the entire time talking to no one in particular about what he would've done if he were there. The flaws in the ammunition they chose. The discreet colors of their camouflage gear that he loves so much. He even models his entire wardrobe by the flat color scheme but amps it up: highlighter colored camouflage shirts: yellow and orange and lime green. His narrating the movies can be kinda annoying really because I'm the kind of person who actually likes to watch a movie, to hear every word that's being said, but I indulge him, ask follow-up questions, act like I know what he's talking about when he answers them, nod my head up and down and say *yea* or *uh huh* every now and then like I do when I'm halfway paying attention in a classroom. He goes on and on, but I don't mind because I've learned that whenever he's granted the access to inform someone on anything—from the rules of basketball—to how to drive a tractor—to how to properly lift weights, these moments exemplify true excitement in his life, which therefore grants true excitement to my life. So I just listen when he stops mid–war movie rant to tell me to invest in a survival kit that includes a backpack full of weaponry and food, and to be in the process of preparing to secure a safe place in the woods to live when it all goes down. This *it* being the apocalypse when the government decides to go off the grid. No electricity, no water, no anything. He says when he dies I can come live in his house, it's in the middle of the woods—*Texas Chainsaw Massacre* country—and everything is already there. There's pitbulls, there's guns, there's water, there's space and opportunity. He's preparing for the world to end and he thinks I'm too weak to survive it. He's preparing for the world to end. He doesn't know I've been surviving it.

His diagnosis is *severe* or *complex* posttraumatic stress disorder, 100% disabled veteran. 100% disabled veteran just means he showed his ass in public places enough times to convince whoever cuts the checks that he's worth, and ultimately owed them on a consistent basis. His diagnosis makes him scary and he revels in it. So much so that he's skipped the suicidal list and moved seamlessly across the board to homicidal. Because he doesn't keep his mouth closed in situations where he should or his hands to himself in situations where its uncalled for, he tells me he can no longer possess a passport, a gun license, and unfortunately, competent psychiatric assistance. Says he had to cuss one of his therapists out because she kept looking down at her iPad while he talked. My mama used to go to a psychiatrist all the time, but she said she don't like how they try to put words in her mouth. She feels this way about psychiatrists, Oprah's interviewing, and me whenever she's telling me a long story with no concrete ending and I can't help asking what is it she's even talking about. She has PTSD too. 90% disabled veteran. I even use her handicap sticker in Wal-Mart parking lots to prove it. Her diagnosis is borderline hilarious for she doesn't let it define her, but she makes sure to mention it whenever it's convenient. Like every Veterans Day when we go to every restaurant that provides a free meal and stack up on her lunch for the rest of the workweek. She's been shooting for 100% for a couple of years now, but even after working at the VA for 28 years, and even after all of her apparent symptoms of forcefulness, forgetfulness, and injury, they just won't let her have it. Her wounds ain't physical enough. She ain't pale enough. She ain't male enough. The extremities my parents' diagnosis places upon them are supposed to be for their safety and the safety of others, yet these limitations have somehow only led to my not knowing how to protect myself from myself, how to determine what is me and what is them, or failing to identify what has transferred inside my blood. I am terrified something is wrong with my brain, the way it messes things up. I am terrified that maybe all this time it has always been me coming to the surface and I cope with who I am by blaming them.

When I was in my mama's womb, something in her, naturally, slipped inside me. She thinks it's the anthrax. I think it's her face and the bad memory. For over a decade she's been saying how much I need to get tested for Gulf War syndrome. She thinks I yell too much. She tells me *it ain't a day go by that you ain't yelling.* I don't mean to; it's just that people make me. When I feel like I'm being asked a similar question in a different way, or I feel like they're not listening correctly, I get upset. But I don't mean to yell, I don't even realize I'm yelling most of the time, it just comes out that way. And I didn't know yelling was a symptom for a medical diagnosis. Gulf War syndrome is something I thought she made up because she makes up a lot of shit. A lot of words. And gets offended when you tell her they aren't real. Like the time I told her Don Cheadle's name is not pronounced Don *Cha-dall* and she stopped speaking to me for a couple of hours. But according to Wikipedia, Gulf War syndrome exists. It has a pulse. It may be beating under my skin. Gulf War syndrome is a medical condition of fatigue, chronic headaches, skin and respiratory disorders due to a combination of pesticides, vaccines, and other unknown chemicals sleeping in your bloodstream, waiting to attack you through attacking others, I think. I don't really attack others as much as I attack myself with my high expectations, but I get the point. She thinks I got double of what she has in her system because my daddy slipped inside her, and let her tell it, he's way crazier than she is.

So when he wakes up one night like a siren is circling his brain, like he's run out of time, popping his back off of the couch cushion as if his limbs are not flesh, but functions, I am not entirely afraid. As he stares around the room, I can tell he doesn't know where he is. I get it; I never know where I am either, what I'm doing in the spaces I occupy ever. He doesn't know who I am or how I got into his home, he just sees my figure sitting on the opposite end of this deep brown wraparound couch under a blanket too fluffy to really keep me warm. I just see him searching for something familiar. The sound from the TV becomes obsolete as his face becomes the screen I'm studying. Even in the dim light, his brightness sticks out. His eyes are wide and red. Weed red or crazy red, I'm not sure. Well-rested red or get the gun behind the big recliner chair red, it all looks the same to me, I don't know, but the moles that circle his face move in closer around his eyes like they're trying to send me a message. Near me there's a lamp, a remote control, another gun at the door—I sit with a multiple-choice question inside my head. He blinks his eyes as fast as a camera shutter in my direction. No sound is loud enough, accurate enough in its intention. I wave at him and say *hey.* I need him to see that it's me, his child, so I say *hey,* again, louder, *you want me to turn the TV down?* I'm working on what to say and how to say it.

There have been many things written about genetic trauma. What it means. What it entails. What it doesn't. I think it means a field knife has slept under my mama's mattress everywhere we've ever lived. Just in case intruders invade our one-bedroom apartment. She has these dreams, I know, because she tells me. She is always dying, or about to die, or about to kill me. Normal mornings are about listening to how a coalition of killer monkeys with human faces came into the house and tied us up in the living room and how she tried to sacrifice herself but the human-faced killer monkeys wanted me and they said she had to be the one to do it and she was about to but then she woke up. Both of them are always dying. Even after they separate and move to different cities and sleep in separate beds, and even after they divorce, and even when I go from a child to a twentysomething—they've always had death—and me—in common. My presence becomes a trigger when I'm with my daddy in Houston and a reminder when I'm home with my mama in Dallas. My entire makeup is like a warning. My parents both tell me that yes, it may be something wrong. I may have inherited a psychological damaging I cannot explain as binding, something I cannot pinpoint the symptoms of, they keep seeing it in the way I fail to exist.

On a car ride, my daddy turns down the music and asks me how am I doing with my depression, something I didn't even know I had, but he seems concerned, and if he sees it I guess that means I might have it, so I say I'm good and only really get sad when I'm about to start my period but I think that's everybody. I don't know everybody, but I am worried that drugs do not work on me. The ones that are supposed to calm me down, ease my anxiety, make me less angry, all make me feel the same. I've tried weed in various forms. The joint. The bong. The edible. And nothing. The Valium does nothing. It all does nothing. I'm self-medicating three to five times a week to go to sleep. I'm having consecutive dreams of being attacked by birds, by pigeons. They see me coming, walking down the street, and they give me their wings. Except they don't let me fly, they weigh me down. I keep having death dreams. I'm not dying but the ship I'm in is sinking. I am taking some of my last breaths. I wake up in the middle of the night and I see bombs detonating under my blanket. When I'm ten, give or take a year, I write a letter to myself about how I want to die. My mama finds it in our bunk bed or my book bag or somewhere else in the small vicinity we share. It says something about hating myself because I love boys so much. It says something about how my family thinks I'm fast because I love the attention of boys so much. I'm being dramatic. I don't mean any of it, but it feels like I could make myself believe it if I wrote it down enough times, so I never claim anyone in public and stay single the rest of my life.

Trying to get black folks to take mental illness seriously is a battle. They think it's a white people disease. They think if something is wrong with the lining of your brain, your body, you don't talk about it. You just need to pray it away. To fix it yourself. So those boxes of pills that are delivered to their front door every week are left unopened. Codeine, Prozac, Paxil, all kinds of unused antidepressants stock dresser drawers unless my mama feels the spirit of giving and shares them. But still, there's so many that could probably help them. My daddy's back has been cut into. His groin swells. His hips are cracking as if he gave birth to me. He lives on all fours. My mama's knees are knocked out of place. Her arms are sore. When you touch her—her bones break due to her fibromyalgia, and I'm just me, playing copycat to their history. We all stay broken and are all good at breaking.

My mama tells me her nightmares started coming while she was still in the tent with my daddy. After they met in the Middle East in a war zone. After a Scud missile hit their mess tent. After they had to scramble for their gas masks. After they fell in the sand together—fell in love—leaned on one another because they thought they were gonna die. I think they fell into a dependency, a kind of desperation; but they endured Desert Storm up into the Texas heat and sometime after this, they had me. And these dreams just spiraled into the bed they shared when they came back home.

I go to visit my daddy. I'm grown now and I stay there close to a month. We've been in the house about two weeks. Normally I wouldn't mind but I feel like making plans for once. I tell him my plans. The next morning he wakes me up at 7:30 a.m. Says I need to be ready by eight. I'm not ready by eight because I'm not a morning person and everyone knows that. He's already in the car by eight. He's blowing his horn like I am a deer in his headlights. I'm just brushing my teeth. I can hear the door of his truck slamming as I spit my bad breath out into the sink. He storms back in and screams, bangs on the door, says we ain't going no more and I hear the volume of SportsCenter get louder. Ten minutes later he knocks on the bathroom door, softer this time, and apologizes. For yelling or rushing me, I'm not sure. I'm calmly putting my contacts in. He says if we're going, we have to leave now. We're rushing through life and I don't know why. I know how he is but I'm getting angrier and I don't know why. I know I act this same exact way when my plans go off schedule, yet him doing it won't allow me to see myself in his actions. We leave the house at 8:15 a.m., catch the first movie showing at nine, leave the bookstore by noon, leave his mother's house by two, and we're back at the house by four. He stays in the car at the bookstore and calls me every five minutes to ask am I done. He stares at the exit sign and fidgets the entire movie. He starts a disagreement with his mother. When we get back home his face turns red again when he looks at me. This is what I've learned: not crazy red but the embarrassed kind of red, like he's sorry to be saying this but he has to when he tells me I'm wrong for making him do this. Things he didn't want to do. He says it's not right of me to come into his space and disturb it. He says I shouldn't come to his house at all if I expect him to be my chauffeur. I just expect him to be my father. I don't stay out late at night.

I'm like 13 when I decide to wear sandals in low 60-degree weather even though my mama told me to put on shoes. I am standing outside the car holding onto the door handle hoping she unlocks it before she gets close enough to see. I've always been good at hiding things. I was a sneaky child and an even more private adult. All I hear is *kendra didn't I tell you . . .* and immediately, my go-to reflex is to duck, to try to outmaneuver my mama's blows. She grabs my right arm and twists my hand behind my back. My palm almost touches the back of my skull. All my fingers are pushed backward until I think they are about to pop off and crawl under the car. She continues to bend and break both of us down to the cement until I am on my knees facing the ground in the parking lot of Saltgrass. This is what I've learned: she means to do it. It looks like she is performing a wrestling move on me. She proceeds to put her elbow in the small of my back and I promise, I'm not even crying. I'm just on the ground thinking she's about to take my arm straight out the socket and feed it to me. There is a crowd watching us and all I'm thinking are these white people gone call CPS on my mama. My cousin, after laughing, finally runs over and saves us *Aunt Carla! Aunt Carla you can't be doing all that in front of these people!* and she lets me go. I ask her does she remember this and she says that's what I get for being disobedient. I don't go outside unless I have to.

I don't want to pass along all the stuff that has been passed down to me.

My mama rushes into the middle of my pre-K classroom, scoops me from the semicircle I sat in and runs out of the door. It was midday. It looked like she was kidnapping her own child. I can remember her going 100 miles per hour on a city street and I can remember my daddy in the truck behind us, chasing us. I can remember him catching us. I can remember him on the right side of our car because I am looking directly into his face, he sees me, but he doesn't. They never do. I can remember him screaming into our window to pull over. I can remember him almost running us off the road in his black rusty pickup. I can remember thinking maybe today would be the last day we ever had to be together as a family, and I was thankful. Because I knew if the three of us continued to breathe the same air, we would cause an explosion.

When a woman is 28 years old, she gives birth to a daughter who grows up angry about things her parents think she shouldn't be angry about. They don't see why, or how she's made their experiences her own stories to tell. They don't even remember her being there until she mentions she was. That she saw. That she witnessed. They tell her they did their best. This is what she's learned: nobody knows what they're doing when war veterans come home, especially the war veterans themselves. The daughter was born making sure not to say the wrong thing, making sure not to make the wrong move. They never have to watch the way they say things because that's just who they are. Sorry becomes a fluent language whether she's done something wrong or not. Whether she was there or not. When she's older, whether she chooses to back down or not. She was a good child. She could be a better daughter.

It is a sunny Sunday morning, I'm a real child, six years old maybe and my daddy doesn't want us to leave the house. My mama gets me dressed in ruffled white socks and an ugly dress with an unnecessary amount of flowers on it, takes me out to the car anyways. We are going to church. We are always going to church. My daddy comes rushing out of the house after us, grabs her wrist to free the car keys from her grip. I just stare as she raises her right foot off of the concrete and rams her heel into his bare feet. They both scream, him in pain, her telling me to get in the car. He lets go of her wrist and the keys fall to the floor. She grabs them and again, we are on the run. I know they've been through more traumatic things than war. They have outlived and outgrown one another. We do not go to our normal church; she knows he will show up there. Instead we go to an old Baptist church in South Dallas. We sit in the pew closest to the door. We stay for what feels like a whole day. I don't pray once. I think my mama has never stopped praying about where to put all our stuff. When we finally return home later that day, my mama's dead father's plant that had grown around all four walls of their bedroom is ripped from its place. Their jungle feels like a desert. It's dry, it's dying. The soil is on the floor, everything in the room is on the floor, broken, torn, the dirt is festering, remembering the days the roots kept it alive. My daddy is in the back room in a brand new mood. My mama goes in to confront him; she's always been a confronter. He's the lion but she's the lion too. They push and shove until she surrenders. I'm there too—watching—but they do not see me. I think the last thing they ever truly saw clearly was each other and bombs that caught fire.

ACKNOWLEDGMENTS

I don't believe in vision boards but I made one for 2018 because I was bored and at home on New Year's Eve. On it, it had dumb shit I wasn't gonna accomplish like gaining upper body strength, learning to draw, and having clear skin. Anyways, on it, I also put "get published." I would explain all the anxiety and rejection that is involved in this process but for the sake of these acknowledgments, all imma say is vision boards are still stupid but here we are.

Of course I have Kiese Laymon to thank, who's the author of one of my favorite books in the world. I still can't believe you're the one who gave this all the green light. Thank you. I'm a forever fan.

Also thank you to the students in the MFA program at Iowa who also had a say in my winning. When I found out, I was absolutely sure that if I won, no one else must have submitted, but I'm so grateful ya'll saw potential in me making everything a black issue and thought maybe other people should read it too. This day forward I'm no longer salty about not getting into the nonfiction program. Thank you. Thank you. Thank you.

Thanks to everyone at the University of Iowa Press for helping me navigate what needed to be done and for printing it out for the public to consume and criticize.

To every workshop peer and professor I've ever had in both Chicago and Alabama who has ever read or listened to me read versions of these essays and told me what parts were trash and what parts could withstand the test of revision, thank ya'll. Thank you to Bobby Biedrzycki's Story and Performance class, which taught me the importance of being able to write a story with intention and conviction. Special thanks to Kathie Bergquist, Re'Lynn Hansen, and Jenny Boully in whose classrooms many of these essays began to take shape. Thank you for being amazing at your jobs and always taking time out to give me your writer wisdom and direction, honestly and with vision. I can't say how much I appreciate it.

Thanks to the following publications for publishing earlier versions of the some of the essays included in this volume: *Harpur Palate* ("Father Can You Hear Me"), *Brevity* (excerpt from "Full Service"), *Habitat Magazine* ("The Cheapest Casket"), *December Magazine* ("When You Learn the Alphabet"), *Hair Trigger* ("Full Service"), *Five:2:One Magazine* ("Mama Said on Motherhood"), and *The Rumpus* ("How To Workshop N-Words").

Thank you to any family, friend, or foe who has ever encouraged, published, shared, or taken the time to read my writing. So much love I don't deserve. And to anyone who actually spent their hard-earned money on this book, so much love I don't think my body is capable of deserving. I appreciate all ya'll.

To *The Friend Zone* podcast—ya'll really do help me with my musty ass brain every single week. Episode 106, "Let Go of The Story," came out when I realized I was tired of regurgitating the same stories over and over but didn't know how to stop because I used them to define myself. Thank ya'll for talking through your own stories, for making me laugh and think, and for teaching me don't nothing grow in a cycle.

All the writers who have made me throw your books across the room and sit in silence because a sentence you wrote fucked me up and made me want to write one of my own. Sistah Souljah. bellhooks. Cherrie Moraga. James Baldwin. Eric Jerome Dickey. Sung Yim. Danez Smith. Toni Morrison. Kiese Laymon. Hilton Als. Amiri Baraka. Vivian Gornick. Jesmyn Ward. Ashley and JaQuavis. Edwidge Danticat. Hanif Abdurraqib. Zora Neale Hurston. Thank you for so many words that will stick with me forever.

Solange's "God Given Name." Raury's "God's Whisper." The entirety of Amy Winehouse's *Frank.* Isaiah Rashad's verse on "Fake Trill." "Ha" by Juvenile. Banks's "Brain." Vince Staples's "45." Outkast's "She Lives in My Lap," which may be the greatest song ever recorded. Mac Miller's live version of "The Question." Jhene Aiko's *Sailing Souls* mixtape. Maxwell's "Submerge: Til We Become the Sun." "Family Portrait" by Pink. "Just Because" by Devin the Dude. Erykah Badu's "Out My Mind, Just in Time." Wayne's "Upgrade U" freestyle. "Civilian" by Wye Oak. And "I Hate U Bitch" by Z-Ro. Ya'll too, have had me in awe of how you use language. Thank you.

And if I never get this chance again, here's to the only things that matter. Dallas, Texas. I hope I make you proud because I'm most proud to be a product of you. You made me brave and loud and inspired. DDD. Texas forever. To my mama and my daddy, I'm even prouder to be a product of ya'll. I hope ya'll are proud of me too, even if I told what you think is just ya business. To the realist nigga on my team, my dog Zero, who sat at my feet all the nights I sat at the computer and pretended to write. And most important, thanks to God, who if I fail to mention, my mama might slap me. Thank you God for all the signals you've given me and the overflow of grace when I didn't follow them.

I never want to see these essays again. They belong to ya'll now.

—Kendra

IOWA PRIZE FOR LITERARY NONFICTION

China Lake:
A Journey into the Contradicted Heart
of a Global Climate Catastrophe
by Barret Baumgart

For Single Mothers Working as Train Conductors
by Laura Esther Wolfson

When You Learn the Alphabet
by Kendra Allen